THE MY STORY, MY JOURNEY:
COLLATERAL BEAUTY

The
My Story,
My Journey:
Collateral
Beauty

**Sandi D. Johnson
& Contributing Co-authors**

First Printing, 2019

ISBN 978-1-7331126-0-4

Published by: EnVision Your Life, L.L.C.

Printed in the United States of America

Acknowledgments

I have never been great at spelling, and this made it difficult for me to be a good writer. At my house, Thursday nights were a struggle growing up. We would sing, rap, write, and dance to my spelling words, only for me to barely pass the test. In college, I would procrastinate when assigned a paper.

Early this year, I tried that same strategy with "Grace to Recover," and the visionary Shirley LaTour was not having it. She pushed that not-so-well-written chapter out of me. I got texts about past due deadlines. These were followed up with direct messages and e-mails. She was relentless at cracking open my writing. It was at the book signing that I expressed my fear, and she understood the push that was required to get my one 2500-word chapter. I thank you Shirley LaTour for that help.

A few years ago, I expressed to my author-friend, MeLisa Collins, that I could not write. I sent her something I had written to read. It was at that point, she informed me I would never say that statement again. She has been my editor and can take my sometimes not-so-well-written thoughts and fix them to make sense.

So, when God gave me the project "My Story, My Journey: Collateral Beauty" (Yes; a whole book! Did I mention that I have another book on single parenting written but not released?), fear almost stopped this project. On this morning, I received the last chapter from someone I had to give the same push Shirley had to do for me. She had submitted one chapter, but I never said much. That chapter was not complete. God fixed it without a word from me. She came and said she needed to do a rewrite. This morning when I spoke to her upon, re-reading her section, do you know what happened? Yes, she received a release and breakthrough. I recall the late great Elder Nick S. Edward, Sr., pastor of New Testament COGIC, saying, "When you can talk about something, healing has taken place." So, I guess that applies to writing too.

This book is doing what it was purposed to do, which is help us embrace the ugly parts of life to identify the beauty.

Foreword

by MeLisa Samia Collins

June 25, 1991 my life was forever changed—just coming off of a high from high school graduation and preparing for entry to college in the fall. This day started as a simple date, though would eventually end my impression of some of the simple innocence of life. I would no longer look at the world through rose-colored glasses and teenage wonder. Just like that, I was afraid! My life before this day was by far a silver spoon-fed walk in the park.

Raised in an inner-city community, surrounded by crime, I was subjected early in life to many of life's downturns—including drugs, gangs, and death. I lost my first childhood friend at 12 years old to gun violence. Despite all of this, I cannot recall ever being "afraid" growing up. On that day, I had been made afraid of what else could happen and what else was lurking around each new corner of my life. I recall riding the bus to work and thinking everyone on it knew what had happened to me. I felt exposed to the world with no way to disappear.

Though time would past, and physical injuries would heal, the emotional wounds festered. I cried, withdrew, quit my job, and cried some more. I found myself going back in my mind to visit the events of that day and obsessively reminiscing over what had gone so tragically wrong and why. How did I allow myself to become prey? Why was I now this victim? What could I have done differently? What was the purpose of this pain?

That was it! Just as I had been so rapidly thrown into being afraid, I was freed by knowing there had to be a purpose for this pain! I had gone through a traumatic and life-changing event; yet, I had survived. There must be a reason for me making it through mentally and physically intact. My memories of that night would eventually become my screenplay, so I would never forget why this experience was given to me. Before this happened, I made choices along my path that lead me to the night of June 25, 1991. When I hit the metaphorical "Brick Wall," that experience forced me to stop and reassess where my life was going and, after conquering my fears, I chose to use my pain for a purpose.

We all have experiences in our lives that cause us pain, and the pain is there for us to evoke what lesson is in this to acquire. This pain is not to hinder our growth, but to give importance to what Pain was trying to teach us. The stories you are about to read are the screenplays of the women who too found the Purpose of their Pain. Each one finds a way to overcome the pain she encountered during her own life's pain, turmoil, bereavements, and hurts and chose bravely to share these stories with the world.

Contents

Introduction

Collateral Damage is a military term which refers to the death of innocent people, or the loss of property during a military action. It results in the innocent suffering due to a situation beyond their control. Many times in life, we experience such circumstances where we are just bystanders to life taking its natural course. Death is one of those times, and we are left with hurt and grief.

In 2016 there was a movie out called *Collateral Beauty* with Will Smith as the lead. The film was about him losing a child and the pain he experienced as the result of this loss. He was an innocent bystander to an illness that claimed the life of his daughter and only child. He falls deeply into grief like many do when the reality hits that we will never physically touch that person again. All the plans for the future like college, wedding, and children have come to an everlasting halt.

In 2000-something, my plans came to an everlasting halt over and over again. I say 2000-something because the mind has a way of blocking out memories to protect the heart. That period is a blur, as I cannot recall dates or details. It started in about March when after a long brave fight against cancer, my stepfather succumbed to it. His death was followed by my mother's death on December 1st.

The day my mother died, my grandfather announced he would be leaving us soon. He was always a man true to his word. Just when I did not think I had any more tears to cry, he slipped away to Glory on February 15th while heading to Bible study.

Being a single parent, these three people were a big part of my support system; my stepfather would come to fix my car and not even fuss when all it needed was gas. My mother was my everything, and she would help make the ends that failed to come together meet. And my grandfather was a Godly man, loved his family unconditionally, and provided me with words of wisdom, credit for cars, a place to live, and the list could go on for days. It was as if a rug of support was pulled out from under me and I was left in midair, but Jesus caught me before the fall.

Now, in *Collateral Beauty,* Will Smith's character wanted an explanation for this tragic loss, so he wrote Time, Love, and Death for answers which he received. When reflecting on these three deaths in a 16-month period, I had my own experience with Love, Time, and Death. My grandfather represented Time as he was blessed to pour wisdom into four generations. He lived a long, blessed life from serving in WWII to seeing the new millennium and beyond. It would seem that God even honored his requested time to return home.

Now, my stepdad was Love, as he showed love towards my mother until his dying breath. During his illness, he kept on filling up the house with groceries. My mother would fuss about all the food they could not possibly eat. Being the good daughter that I am, I would swing by the house and take some of that food off their hands. Yes, I was helping them out by taking bags of groceries home. Later, I realized he was trying to provide for her after he was no longer physically here. When he was transitional, according to my sister, he did not take his last breath until she assured him that we would care for her. It was here that I realized love extended beyond the grave. Love provides provisions for those they love.

Lastly, my mother was Death. Her leaving here, as painful as it was, brought about the death of my current lifestyle; it was my catalyst. Remember how Love provided provision for those they love? My mother did just that. Those provisions were used to leave Detroit, MI and relocate to Texas. The move enabled me to start a career in education and to be able to make my ends meet independently. It was the death of surviving and the beginning of living life on purpose.

So, as I encounter my own Time, Love, and Death, I embrace the Collateral Beauty of them all. I celebrated the blessing—while struggling through the lessons—all the while finding a strength I never knew I possessed.

This book is a journey into thirteen brave women's stories and the lessons, blessings, and strength they gained from their experiences. These are stories of them embracing their Collateral Beauty.

Chapter 1
Stay Woke

by Shaundale Rénā

#DontCommit2Crazy

It's taken some time to sit and steady myself for this project. From topic to topic, week to week, I have considered my options over the past couple of months. The one that resonates most is a lesson I learned a few days ago: the first 40 years of my life are collateral; the last five are simply beautiful. Why? How could that be? It's simple. When you spend your life trying to accommodate everyone else, you're not true to you. If you're not true to you, you're not living. If you're not living, then you must be dying. See. Simple. So, I'll just be reclaiming the next 45 years if the Lord lends them to me. And, I hope you're paying attention because I'm making good on each one.

Where do I start? How did it begin? Ah, here we go. Being a good student came easily to me. So did being a good person. I was a quiet child who was smart, respectful, and sincere. I was the one people knew would go to a good college, get a good job, marry a good man, live in a good neighborhood, drive a good car, raise a good family, and live a good life. For all intended purposes, I was a "good" child with a "good" and bright future. You won't hear me complain about any of the expectations placed on me—although unrealistic it would seem looking back—because I was taught to do as you're told. So, I've almost always been the one to do so—even to my own detriment. Went to a good school. Check. Got a good job. Check. Married a good man, lived in a good neighborhood, drove a good car, raised a good family, and lived a good life? All highly questionable and very suspect. "Good" is in the eye of the beholder.

Having "been there, done that" grew old quickly. I'd graduated from Grambling State University, landed my first post-college job at Burlington Northern Santa Fe Railway, and started the journey of my "good life" all easily and seemingly effortlessly. Thinking back, it appears plenty came easily for me. If I studied, I'd earn an A+; if I didn't, I'd earn a B. (Shrugs shoulders.) Then college happened. Along with it came pledging, parties, and programs for one community club or another I was not only a member of, but an officer in as well. If I studied, I'd earn a B; if I didn't, I'd earn a C. (Shrugs shoulders again.)

What happened? I got tired. It seemed there was always something else to accomplish... still more to achieve. Life would never just "be" is the only way to describe it now. It simply became this robotic, monotonous experience that

I sauntered into and out of every 24 hours. I'd done well, but I wasn't good. I was in a place where I needed more to sustain me, and money wasn't it—neither was my car, nor my residence. I needed something I couldn't attain on my own; something that would steady me, not leave me wanting more after another achievement. It was like I was living just to get, do, or have. I wanted to be. Be what? I didn't know. It just had to be more than educated, more than employed, more than okay. It had to make me happy.

· I remember going through months of disappointments. I lost all joy for my "good job" and my new career. Matter-of-fact, I was coming and going—not even remembering getting from one place to another. Sleep-walking, sleep-driving, probably sleep-living. Yeah, I'm pretty sure of it now. There were days I'd park my car at work and hadn't remembered driving. I'd gotten up, gotten dressed, gotten in the car, gotten on the highway, gotten to work, and parked. And truth be told, some of us are living our "good life" in that same zombie-like state right now. Newsflash... #WakeUp

I hated to do that to some (the not-ready-yets) and loved it for others (the ready-to-gos and don't-know-hows). Again, one more time, in your best Lawrence Fishburne voice as if we're all in *School Daze*: Wake up! You see, I'd gotten to that place where I'd been brainwashed into believing all I had to do to create the life I wanted was to go to school, finish college, get a job, make good money, get married, and life would be good. So, in that order, I set out to be good. Only problem was... I wasn't.

So, according to the expectation, what did I do next? I got married. Think about it; goal after goal, expectation after expectation, I was living as if life was a sprint I had to complete to get somewhere just long enough to race again. With just enough time in between each competition, I rested long enough to begin a new chapter. From marriage to children, from children to motherhood, I'd awake just enough to fall back into an even deeper sleep and a heavier zombie mode. Dead wife; dead life. How 'bout that?

It took me years to realize how far I'd gone under. Like an agent working a case, I'd been so deeply "undercover" I'd managed to fool myself. I'd avoided detection as the walking dead for nearly a decade by assuming the identity of a happy wife and a fulfilled mother for the purposes of completing yet another task. Just one more thing to do, one more goal to achieve. When would it stop, and where would it end? It wouldn't. Because, when you are used to competing with yourself to make others proud, you find your purpose in your next position. I'd graduated from high school with five scholarships. I'd graduated from college with six job offers. I'd graduated from career wife to stay-at-home mom. There was nothing else to do. I'd reached the highest calling: motherhood. And, I still wasn't happy. The zombie had awakened long enough to give birth to new hopes and new dreams for a family.

However, she had no way to measure new ideas and aspirations of her own. Consumed with the daily ideals (and inconveniences) of family life, I woke up one last time to birth a book 11 years into my marriage and slept for years to come.

As the words "collateral beauty" resonate in my mind, I wonder at what point I awoke and how long I was out. I missed so much during that time, I've had to remind my family I wasn't here for this, that, and the other. I literally lost myself in the shadows of everyone else. My marriage was the face of the family. The kids were the hands, arms, legs, and feet. We went where they went. We did what was necessary: track, soccer, gymnastics, dance, drama, orchestra, volleyball, PTA, etc. I'd lost so much of myself staying home in this season, running around in that one, I forgot who I was. I'd ask myself, "Aside from being Mama and Honey, who are you?" (Shrugs shoulders again.)

I don't know. (Shrugs shoulders some more.) That did it for me. I'd had enough. I'd put my life on hold, although no one had asked me to, far longer than I'd considered. If I had to do it again, I'd go back to work after about six months. Six weeks, in my opinion, is too little time to give new parents. It's also too little time to give a newborn. But, even still, I'd take my six months and resume my goal-chasing with a new perspective. My original one only included me attaining mountaintop after mountaintop just to be able to say I'd done it. My new one would include me attempting to balance my career and my family to be able to say I'd done it. Same result, different approach. And, I'd probably have found my joy much sooner.

Speaking of joy... it took a while to get here. The first few years of marriage were a honeymoon. The next few were okay. Nothing magical happened. We bought a house, had two daughters, and figured the rest out. We did "normal people" stuff. To this day, if you didn't know we've had problems, you wouldn't know we've had problems. Fast forward a decade, and I've authored two books and collaborated on two more. In fact, I've started working again. Honestly, by that time, I was all over the place because I lacked the focus from my single, childless season of chasing dreams and setting goals. It was me trying to catch up to myself. Never have I stopped competing with me. Except when I went into zombie mode. And I'd been "under" so long, I was buried alive before I knew it. Years passed and I watched myself play catch up. I wrote; I worked; I ate; I slept; I breathed. None of which needed me to be fully awake. It wasn't until I got the wake-up call of my life that I was shocked back into an existence I wasn't even aware existed anymore.

As a wife and mother, I had done what one person had warned me never to do: lose my identity. It was an older lady from my last job from which I'd taken FMLA and later resigned who'd told me to stay independent, but

I'd done the total opposite. Surely, my husband would provide for and protect me; certainly, my children would need me. Surely. Certainly. Well, my husband provided for and protected me from myriads of truth, and my children outgrew needing bathwater run and clothes picked out. My marriage was as crooked as the next, and my children were as confused as anyone else's.

Truth be told, I was only blindsided by my own inhibitions. I compared myself to friends who hadn't married and were building their careers. I compared myself to friends who had married, and yet had no children and were strengthening their relationships. I even compared myself to friends who had married, started a family, and divorced. All I wanted was hope—and a future all my own. Sure, I'd share it with them once profits were rolling in; however, the process and the project were my own. In short, I needed something to do that was mine and mine alone—something that didn't have to do with the family, the children, or the house. Just me.

When it finally dawned on me that I was struggling with separation anxiety *from myself*, I had lost it. Literally. I spent 18 months with a therapist that I attribute to saving my life. As a result of spending that time with her, I woke up and changed my life. If you don't want to do something, you find something else to do, right? Well, that's what I did.

When I was single, I'd travel like an airline stewardess. So, that's the first thing I did. I took a trip to Atlanta— my first time back in 18 years. (In this moment, I realize the symbolism of the 18 months and the 18 years.) I also packed a bag and headed to Houston, San Francisco, or anywhere else I could afford to go... by myself. "The dead is arisen," as Old Mister said in Alice Walker's *The Color Purple*. It felt good to be able to recognize myself. I'd started living again, dressing up again, going to the hair and nail salon again, and believing in myself as more than someone's wife or mother again. Screw that. Wifedom nor motherhood are anyone's singular purpose. I doubt highly that God created *me* just to oversee other people's life goals. No indeed.

Knowing fully well now that I'd gone from life to death over the course of the last 20 years, there is plenty that I can look back over and say, "Aha" for. From infancy up until middle-agedom, I have been able to connect the dots and see where one person, place, or phrase planted seeds of deliverance or doubt. I was the one who was going to go out into the world and "be" somebody. I was going to "do" something. I was the one who if anybody was going to "make it," I was. The things spoken into or over my life weren't my own to manifest.

They were God's. I found myself rushing His timing and running quarterback with His plans. I'd done so much to set my own self up to succeed that I couldn't handle failure. And, it showed. Gone were the days of breezing through classes and blindly dashing through life. I now had to put in the work, and it was hard. I'd done okay as a wife, but I have—by no means—arrived. I've done well as a mom, but there is always room to grow. I hit a wall with both. I had sacrificed my life for the greater good of everyone else—unasked—and had paid a price I couldn't be refunded, nor did they owe me. So, when I woke up... believe me, I woke up.

It's kind of hard to reflect on all this now. In the same sense, it's also rather astonishing. Who gets to die and live again? However, I am different. I have always been. That's part of the reason why "normal" wasn't working for me. It was "normal" to get married. It was "normal" to start a family. It was "normal" to sacrifice my dreams. Normal takes on a whole new meaning when you add two letters: A and B.

Yes; abnormal is a real word... and quite a good one if you're like me. I am abnormal. That doesn't mean I'm crazy. It simply means, in most instances, I will be atypical and unconventional in my thinking. I am also artistic. That does mean I might be a little special (just a little). Okay, I'm kidding. But, on the real, all creatives are a little thrown off. That's why I can see and say now that I slept my way through life up to a certain point; the point where I refused to not be me anymore.

With every major transition, I became more and more comatose. I finished high school. Yay. I finished college. Yay. I started a career. Yay. I got married. Yay. I gave birth... three times. Yay, yay, yay. In retrospect, none of that mattered after awhile. Where was I? Where had I gone? And, how could I get me back? Yeah, that part— that whole part.

This year I told God if He would get me back to a "right" place of mind, I would make the necessary decisions. I promised that 2019 would be the year I focused on me, and everyone else would have to sit back and watch. And, so far, I've done what I set out to do. Because, I decided to stay woke.

Collateral Beauty Moments

Being a parent, I can relate to the loss of self. Has there been a time like Shaudale Rénā's experience where you cannot even account for how you arrived at the place where you are? As if you were on cruise control? For years, if someone asked me a simple question about my likes, I drew a blank. Ummm, being a team mom for football or taxicab for my children. Do those count? If you are like me and in the process of reclaiming yourself, Shaudale Rénā Collateral Beauty began by acknowledging the loss. Shaudale Rénā approached life with a checklist created by the expectations of society, family, and self. This created a zombie effect of existing but not living life.

- When you reflect on your life, have there been times when you lost yourself to the expectations of others?

- Have you ever experienced a zombie effect in your life?

- Her turning point was to acknowledge the issues and to go to counseling. How would you know that it was time to seek out help?

- On her journey to reclaim herself, she took a trip. What would be something that might help you on your journey?

We all have had experiences that leave us gasping for air.

Chapter 2
Only by God's Grace
by Dr. Monica Debro
#Love2Life™

"Blessed are those who mourn, for they will be comforted."
Matthew 5:4 (NIV)

As I was preparing for work—one already hot, sunny June 2011 morning in Phoenix, Arizona—I kept having this nudging in my heart to visit my parents. It was early morning, and my initial response was to ignore the nudging and continue with my day as usual. At the time my mother was 79, and my father was 84. My thought was *they're still sleeping and enjoying not having to get out of bed early.* I didn't see a need in my natural thoughts to go over and wake them up.

While my normal routine was to visit them in the evening, this nudging feeling would not go away. I continued to get dressed and think about my plan for the workday. Once I was dressed, I walked out of my bedroom and downstairs to my welcoming kitchen to make a cup of coffee. All the while, I couldn't shake this nudging; this feeling that wouldn't go away to visit my parents before work. As the Keurig was heating the coffee and preparing to make the one drink I started my day with, I turned on the surround sound to play calming praise and worship music.

In the mornings, I preferred songs that provided a calm and comforting feel for praying. I needed to focus quietly on prayer and seek God as I was preparing to start the busy part of the day. Anytime I woke up late or failed to get my clothes together the night before, I was rushed and often didn't spend time in quiet prayer before hurrying out of my home to go to work. Every time this happened, it never failed that the workday had a rushed, "what in the world?" type of feel. I would always feel as though I wasn't getting anything done. On these days, I felt anxious. I felt unorganized. I felt as though my time was out of control. My thoughts would be all over the place, yet no place at all.

As soon as I recognized I hadn't spent my quiet time in prayer and that's why my day was going haywire, I would quickly close my office door, go to YouTube, and play music to spend some quiet time with God. Having a private office allowed me to have this uninterrupted space when I needed to seek God to settle my emotions and anxieties, so that I could hear His voice and have a better day. The quiet time began with me apologizing for not being prepared to spend quality time with Him before leaving home and beginning the rush of my day. From there, I gave thanks to Him and poured out my heart in reverence to His amazing love.

Once I'd placed myself in God's presence, it opened me up to a day that was less hectic and less emotional. I was able to focus, complete tasks, have a true open-door policy to deal with the issues among students, clinical, classes, grades, meetings, etc. I was able to actively listen to others because once again, my thoughts weren't running everywhere, yet nowhere at all. The coffee was ready, and the music was playing; it was time. After putting creamer in the coffee, I picked it up and walked around the stairwell to the prayer room. Of all the rooms in my home, this one had a different level of peace, calm, and quietness to it. It was a room I'd dedicated to devotion time, reading my Bible, praying, writing, and just sitting when I needed to calm whatever emotion was running rampant. I slipped out of my shoes and walked into the room.

The plush carpet was welcoming and felt good on my feet. I've laid prostrate, sat with my legs crossed, kneeled in prayer, cried, and slept on this carpet. I stopped wearing shoes in the prayer room after feeling uneasy several times that I'd gone in for one reason or another. One morning as I was leaving for work, God explained to me why I wasn't to wear shoes in the prayer room. He acknowledged the place as Holy ground. My heart blossomed as He spoke those words to me about the room I'd dedicated to spending time with Him. From that day forward, shoes were not allowed in this sacred space.

I don't remember exactly what I prayed about, the scripture I read, or the songs I listened to that morning, but my time with God was my time with God. I'm always quieted and have that "peace that surpasses all understanding." (Philippians 4:7 paraphrased)

As I left my quiet neighborhood that morning, I made the left turn in obedience to the nudging I'd been feeling. The drive to my parents' apartment was less than 5 minutes, and I was sure my visit would be quick. Since I had a key, I decided to use it and not wake them up. I'd planned to kiss them on the cheek and leave for work. My mother was in the kitchen fixing eggs and sausage for breakfast, and the coffee was already prepared. I gave her a hug and kiss and asked about dad. She responded, "he just walked back to the bedroom." I walked into their room, and the whirlwind began of me switching from daughter to nurse.

Dad was halfway in the bed with only his back on the mattress. His arms were firmly drawn up to his chest, knees bent and feet on the floor. He was unresponsive and eyes rolled back into his head. In response to me calling my dad in a loud and commanding voice, my mother ran into the room. I asked her to call 911 and proceeded to check his blood glucose (BG) level. Once, twice, three times, the BG didn't register on the monitor. In between checking the glucose level, I'd asked my mother to bring some sugar so I could place it under his tongue. Nothing! He wasn't responding and where in the world was the Emergency Medical Service (EMS) team?

By the time EMS arrived and checked his BG, it was 50. They started an IV and raised his BG to 200; yet, they refused to take him to the hospital, stating he didn't need additional medical care. Of course, I didn't follow their advice. I quickly got dad dressed and drove him to the emergency room, which was a 15-minute drive. By the time we got there and they checked his BG level, it had rapidly increased to 57. He was admitted into the hospital, and a multitude of test were completed. He had several doctors on the team, providing care, and determining the next best plan of care.

As many family members were sitting around Dad's bed laughing and talking, the oncologist walked into the room. Dad was in high spirits and looking forward to being discharged from the hospital. In all of his professionalism, respect, and dignity, the doctor—with calmness and careful attention to his words—provided us with the most imperative diagnosis of liver cancer. He informed us that the life expectancy for our father was six months. Wait; we weren't expecting this new information. Silence filled the room. I looked at Dad's face, and it appeared that the light had gone out of his eyes, as he was processing what the doctor had said. After a few moments, my father's only words to the doctor were, "Well, Doc, you worry about me dying; I'll keep on living." And with that, my father didn't allow the diagnosis to cause him any worry or to change his outlook on life. If he was ever worried or concerned, he never said a word to any of us.

Fast forward to the hot, sunny month of July 2012. My parents decided to move to Arkansas. Yes; my father was still living and enjoying his life over a year after being told he had six months to live. They wanted Arkansas to be their final resting place. Although I wanted to keep them in Arizona for our weekly Saturday outings and all the other shenanigans we would get into, I honored their wishes.

While I have a small belief that my mother knew her health status before moving from Arizona, she became very ill and was hospitalized in August 2012. She, too, had cancer and was dealing with this disease erupting in her body. We don't know exactly when my mother was diagnosed, but when we found out, she'd declined rapidly. I went to Arkansas to be with her and spent several days providing care for her. There were days in which she was in less pain and we could get her out of bed to sit in a chair. On other days, we turned her every two hours while in bed to prevent skin breakdown. The last day I saw my mother alive was some months prior on my birthday. My sister had taken our father to the hospice area of the hospital for a visit. He prayed with her and sang songs as his way of comforting his loving wife. An hour later, on my sister's birthday, my mother had transitioned from life to death and was (as she'd always been) in the arms of the Father. During the time of my mother's illness, our father had tripped on a floor rug, broken his pelvic bone, been hospitalized, and transferred to the rehabilitation center. When I visited him in August, we sat in the dining room while he ate a meal I'd taken that he'd requested. He looked at me with sad eyes and asked me not to leave him at the rehabilitation center. In his mind, he was in a nursing home and not in rehab to help him gain strength and heal from the pelvic injury. I was sad when I left him, but I knew it was best for the time being.

Several days after my mother's funeral, two suitcases were packed for my father, and he boarded a plane to move to Carsen, California with one of my sisters. While in California, he was established in hospice care. When the nurse asked him about his goal, my father boldly and confidently responded: "I want to go to Disneyland." We weren't surprised because he was determined to keep moving, to stay active, and to enjoy life to the fullest.

Several times a week, I would receive pictures of Dad at different places such as: Knott's Berry Farm and the Butterfly Farm. He was going to ice cream parlors, restaurants, and the beach or anywhere else he requested, or my sister and nephew suggested. Determined to keep moving, they were always going somewhere. After two months of going to visit him in California, his health began to decline. Here I was, in the midst of experiencing another parent beginning the transition from life to death.

Thankfully, the Director and faculty at the college were very understanding because there were weeks when I would be in California caring for him. I was advised to apply for Family Medical Leave of Absence (FMLA) and was quickly approved. If he was in the hospital, I was at his bedside. When he was discharged, and transferred to my sister's home, I was at his bedside. No matter what else was going on in my life, I was Daddy's girl and needed to be with him.

On Tuesday, November 6, 2012, President Barack Obama was elected for a second term. We celebrated with my father as he was still here to witness history. On Sunday, November 11, 2012, our brother Rev. Walter L. Debro, Jr. was elected pastor of the St. John M. B. Church, a church my father founded years before retiring. By this time, our father was unresponsive; yet, we called our brother and placed the phone to our father's ear so he could give him the good news. On Monday, November 12, 2012, our father transitioned from life to death and was (as he'd always been) in the arms of the Father.

Now, you may think that both of my parents passing was enough for me to experience emotionally within a short period. Well, while witnessing what was happening with my parents and helping to provide care for them, I was also in the crux of a divorce. Yes; another significant life change was occurring in the background, and now this quiet storm was soon coming to an end. There wasn't any evidence of me being married with the deaths of our parents—only a simple name change to my maiden name on the obituary for our father.

There was no need to put energy into the impending divorce while taking care of our parents because all of the papers were in the process of being signed and submitted to the courts. There was no need for me to give extra effort to something already dead. I was emotionless in the release of the marriage. On December 12, 2012, my divorce was final and, just like that (in less than four months), I'd had three significant life changes, yet managed to keep going and survive them all.

Dealing with loss has often been different for me because I've not allowed myself to grieve the way I should. I pushed feelings down and realized that most of the time with my parents, I was a nurse instead of a daughter. There were many questions from others about how I was dealing with the losses and still functioning. I'd learned to focus on God's truth; "The LORD is close to the brokenhearted and saves those who are crushed in spirit." Psalm 34:18 (NIV)

Now that I've shared my story, let's talk about what not to do when someone is dealing with loss, whether it is loss of a loved one or friend, job, home, car, relationship, etc. The two words I despised hearing the most were "be strong." After hearing this from several people, I started to get irritated. Do you realize that when you tell someone to be strong, you're telling them not to feel emotions, not to cry, not to express the feelings of their loss? This is one reason I remained stoic at times throughout everything. People were expecting me to be strong. There were times that I refused to allow a tear to fall; I refused to get emotional. Outside of the wake and funerals for my parents, I did what I was told, "Be strong." I put on the mask that many of us wear: The mask that indicates everything is *all* good.

Everyone will grieve and work through loss differently. So, what do you do when you or someone else is grieving? Below are a few action steps to consider.

Action Steps:

- Grieve your loss. Spend quiet time reflecting on the loss, praying and asking God to comfort you. If the loss is a relationship, job, home, car or something else material, ask God to help you learn the lesson of the loss and grow from it instead of allowing it to catapult you into a world of darkness and the spirit of giving up.

- When you feel like talking, share your thoughts and feelings with someone you trust.

- If you're the one who's been called to be a comfort, understand that words aren't always necessary. Learn to sit, be with the person, and be still.

- Avoid using the words "be strong." Be sincere and allow the grieving person to cry, yell, or express whatever feeling(s) they need toat the moment.

We all grieve in different ways, and that is expected and perfectly fine. What isn't good is when we bottle up those feelings as if we don't deserve to grieve. God is our comfort and as the opening scripture says: "Blessed are those who mourn, for they will be comforted." Matthew 5:4 (NIV) We have every right to mourn and grieve as a result of a loss. Healthy grieving is beneficial. Be honest with yourself about how you're feeling and avoid pretending all is well. Outside of God you're the only person feeling your exact feelings, having your exact thoughts, and who knows what you need to heal from your loss. I want you to allow God to heal your broken heart and bind up your wounds. (Psalms 147:3 paraphrased)

It's only by God's grace that I was obedient to the nudging. It's only by God's grace that I was able to manage the unchangeable moments between August and December 2012. It's only by God's grace that my heart wasn't crushed, and I maintained a spirit of peace.

Although I miss my parents, God's grace gives me pleasant and fun memories. His grace also sends unexpected feelings of their presence close to me and frequent glimpses of them in my dreams. His grace covers, protects, and heals.

Collateral Beauty Moments

Not only did Dr. Monica experience the death of her parents, but also the loss of her marriage. The expression "when it rains, it pours" is all too common in our lives. Just like Dr. Monica found her Collateral Beauty, you can too.

- Are there any areas of your life where you are wearing a mask?

    Many times when there is a death, people say many meaningful words or cliché phases such as: "time heals" and "be strong."

- Does time really heal all wounds?

- What do you think will be the result of someone suppressing their feelings to "be strong"?

- According to Dr. Monica, sometimes your quiet presence is all that is required, can you think of anything else that might help a person grieving?

- If you were in Monica's situation, who are some trusted people in your life whom you can share your feelings with openly and safely?

Chapter 3

A Hero's Legacy

by Danielle Renee'

Losing a precious soul to a senseless, tragic, death at a young age is way too common nowadays. Growing up in a single-parent home in the heart of Detroit, my younger brother, sister, and I had a great upbringing. I was the oldest; my brother was six years younger, and my sister 11 years younger than I. Our mother worked at the local community college for many years until she retired. We knew no lack. She always kept food in the refrigerator, both food pantries in the basement were always stocked, as well as the big deep freezer we had. She taught me how to cook and take care of the house early on in my life. Our mom did not make it a chore; she made it our responsibility, which helped make it fun. She taught her children good work ethic and instilled in us the importance of education.

Being the oldest of the three children, I was the child our mother prepared to care for my younger siblings. I felt

I was their second mother. If they did not do their chores on time, I would remind them. If they did not do their homework, I would remind them. Even when it came down to taking their baths, I would tell them to when our mom was resting or asleep. She structured our house to be a home that produced peace.

On the weekends, our grandparents would come to pick us up along with our cousins and take us up North where we own over 10 acres of land. We enjoyed being up there because it was our get away from the noise in the city. The city life produced sirens, a lot of movement of people walking up and down the streets, loud arguing, kids playing and running in the streets and sometimes gunshots on the constant. Up North, which we considered the country, the lifestyle was stillness and quietness.

Our home sits in front of a lake that is very serene and calm. We had dirt bikes, canoes, sandcastles, and our grandfather built a play yard with a basketball hoop, swings, and a slide. At night my grandfather and uncles would collect wood, so we could have a big barn fire every evening. The barn fire would allow all the family to come together, tell ghost stories, and roast marshmallows. All the kids hated when Sunday came around because we knew it was time to round everything up and head back to the noisy city. We would not fret much because we knew the next weekend was right around the corner. As kids we stayed up North for weeks at a time. We were well-grounded as children and never saw or heard of violence in our family, besides what would be on television.

December 15, 1997 would later change all of that for our family. On that day, the peace we had in our family met violence and we were forever interrupted. My brother, Jason, was tragically struck down by gun violence but died a hero. Mistaken identity was the cause; he was only nineteen years old.

Jason, his girlfriend, his best friend, and his best friend's girlfriend were out that day Christmas shopping at a local mall. He had just called our mother and asked her what to get his dad for Christmas. Her response was, "Get him what you always get him, a pair of socks!" Unknown to my mother that would be the very last time she would ever hear his voice. My brother and his friends left that particular mall and proceeded to the next mall, which was approximately 15 minutes away.

Jason had a sweet, pleasant personality to be around. He was not a troublemaker, and everywhere he went, he made friends. Some of us would always tell him that he was too friendly. He would say to me, "How could I be too friendly? That does not even make sense. I am just being me. Myself. Your little brother, Jay!" He never looked for trouble, but this day trouble found him. The peace he had met violence that day. They left the mall, got in his car, and he told everyone in the car that the same guys in the mall that were causing ruckus seemed to be following them while he was driving.

Jason decided to pull up at a Taco Bell drive-thru in an attempt to lose the guys in the other car. By the time they got their food, he'd thought they were in the clear. Approximately five minutes later, they pulled out of the drive-thru and headed to the other mall. Suddenly, my brother realized the same guys were following them still.

About seven minutes into the ride, Jason told everyone in the car, "Get down, he has a gun!" At the time, he was driving in an underpass of the freeway. He got off the freeway when they all heard the gunshots ringing. It was described that my brother saw the other guys throw up gang signs in his rearview mirror. He was trying to get away but could not. In an attempt to save lives, he did; just not his own. It was one bullet that penetrated his head. Only one shot destroyed our lives forever. He saved the lives of his three closet friends. The senselessness of killing someone is very devastating, and some of us never recover from it. It's bad enough to have to deal with death naturally, but a senseless death is just too much. It makes you feel like you want to die with them. We later found out that the guy who killed my brother was three years younger than he was. Jason's murderer was only a baby himself. He was 16 years old. We learned after the arrested that he shot and killed the wrong person. The guy they were looking for resembled my brother and had the exact color and type of car he had had—a gold, four door, Honda Accord. Come to find out, the guy he was looking for, they had encountered before. The b rother o f J ason's m urderer had shot the other guy before on a basketball court, and that young man still had three bullets in him from that shooting. My brother's murderer ended up getting 15 years. The sentence was not enough time for me. After his arrest, we were in court three weeks straight. Day after day, we had to look at and see the murderer and his family that was acting out in court on some days. Within those three weeks of being in court, the young man whom they mistook Jason for ended up dead. He was set up. The gentleman was at a house party, and one of his so-called friends kept insisting that he needed to go get something out of his car. When he got into his car, someone else was in the back seat of the vehicle and shot him in the back of the head. We found this out one day after court; we were summoned to the police office because the mother of the gentleman who had just been murdered the day before was requesting the reward money that we had put out there in my brother's case. Little did she know, my brother's murderer had already been arrested. She ended up telling his dad she knew the whole story all this time, and that my brother was killed mistakenly. She showed a picture of her son to us. If I had not seen her son in the same car as my brothers, I would have thought he was my very own brother. They resembled each other a lot.

My brother, Jason Minlic Chapman, a hero! My hero! He saved three lives that were in danger of a cold-blooded murderer. He told his friends to get down while speeding up in his car to get away. He was just a second too late.

Jason's lifeless body behind the wheel of his car drifted to the side of the road. There was no crash, either. His girlfriend sitting in the front seat of the vehicle had to reach over his dead body to get his cell phone to call for help. One of the calls would be to my mother to tell her what had just transpired. My mother yelled upstairs to me that my brother had just gotten shot. I immediately fell on the floor of the kitchen and began to pray. I remembered telling God in my prayer if he had to suffer to take him immediately. Do not let him suffer was my request.

I soon got up from the floor, went downstairs, and we headed to the hospital where he died. His dad was out of the state at the time. When we arrived at the hospital, the doctors wanted my mother to identify his body. I would not let her. I did not know the condition of the wound, and I knew I did not want her to see him in that state. I would take that pain any day to ease the pain from our mother. My pastor rushed to the hospital, and he went back there to identify my brother's body with me.

Yes, it was him... my little brother, Jay. I was relieved to see that the bullet wound was not visible for me to see. I was grateful for that.

After the three long weeks in court every day, we finally got to the last day in court. The judge set aside time for the family to speak. I was one of the family members to speak to the entire courtroom. I told everyone by the sound of my voice, from the judge to the court reporter and every family member who was in there, if they did not know God that they had better get to know Him. There is a judgment day that is coming, and we all better be in a rightful place. I told them all that if they were not living right, they had better start living right.

I spoke to my brother's murderer. He never looked up at me while I was talking to him. He appeared not to have any remorse for what he had done and caused. I told him that I prayed that he would get himself together and that I forgave him. I meant every word I said. I forgave my brother's murderer! I know I needed peace in my life, and holding on to the pain of it would do me no good. I knew Jason was a good, young man. He had done no one any harm. I knew he did not deserve for his life to be snatched from him like that. He did not have any children to leave behind, but he will always, always have the lasting legacy of being a hero!!!

Collateral Beauty Moments

Whenever you start something new such as this project, you reach out to your circle, including family. Danielle is not only a co-author but my cousin, and December 15th is a day that will be forever etched in my mind. That day started very "off" for me. I went to work with this feeling in my stomach that usually occurs when I am out of sorts with God. It was a feeling of sadness that I did not know where it was coming from, so I went thru my sin checklist trying to recall what I might have done that was not pleasing to God.

I was exhausted that day and heading straight to bed, but I spent the night tossing and turning. For the life of me, I could not get comfortable. That feeling would not leave. The phone rang, and it was my dad. He asked, "What's Donna's boy's name." I responded "Jason." He said that Jason had just been "shot and killed." I headed straight to the hospital believing that he had to have the name mixed up. This had to be a mistake of some kind. That feeling started to shift and make sense. It had been an alarm that something was shifting and HE had a task for me. It was not something I had done, but something

I would be required to do. Upon arrival at the hospital, a majority of my family was gathering in this small room off to the side in the Emergency Room.

Shortly, I was able to go see Jason. He was laying there as if he was sleeping so peacefully. I rubbed his arm, and it was still warm. He was so warm. And it was as if as I walked in the door Death had just escaped out of it.

My beautiful-spirited cousin was gone. Now, who would I get to help me move at the last minute? Who would I argue with about whether or not Tupac was really dead? Who would teach me about forgiving others?

That was the last conversation I'd had with Jason—about forgiveness and reconciliation. I have a few close family members that I do not always see eye-to-eye with, and we have waves where we do not even communicate or support each other in love. It is not all their fault, nor mine, but a combined effort that had contributed to this dysfunctional relationship. Well, we were in one of our angry waves, and Jason just simply told me, "They are family, and you'll need to stop it." Just simple words of wisdom from my younger, yet wiser cousin.

The forgiveness that Danielle extended Jason's murderer was very indicative of who Jason was and will away be. Has there been a time in your life that forgiveness was required for what some would view as an unforgiveable offence?

Chapter 4
Tell Me How You Really Feel
by Sonya Thomas

After submitting what turned out to be my first draft, Sandi asked, "How do we see the collateral beauty in this story?" I, in return, gave her my fluffy, superficial version. She was okay with my reply, but I really had to think about it. After a few weeks, it hit me like a ton of bricks. In order to know my collateral beauty, you first must understand my collateral damage. I had to come face-to-face with what was my reality... my truth for lack of a better term.

My 17-year-old pregnant mother married my dad to get out of the house, and my 19-year-old father married her because she was pretty. I am sure they loved each other in their own way, but this is what my parents said. It didn't matter that the child she was carrying wasn't his, he was determined to care for his family; they truly did love each other.

What happens when two young, immature, teenagers get married? Yeah, a whole lot of drama. My daddy was a happy-go-lucky, life-of-the-party, everybody's friend type of person. My mom was pretty much the same way. She would cook; he would work, and in-between times they would have fun. Except when they were fighting; those were the times I came to hate my parents. I hated my mom because she didn't know how to shut up. I hated my dad because he didn't know how to walk away. I used to pray for him to die, so the pain of it all would stop.

I remember how one time when they were arguing about something, I laid in my bed praying to God to make her shut up. I knew the result if she didn't. Sure enough, my mother ended up in the hospital with a broken jaw. Now don't think my mother was a punk; she gave as good as she got. Another time my father came home from a party. She was cooking him dinner; he was mad he lost a piece of jewelry at a gambling party. She simply asked, "Are you okay?" He slapped her. She stabbed him in the back. He was in the intensive care for a few days. She was at his side the whole time, and that was the last fight they had. I thought, cool I could get used to this. I didn't know how wrong I was.

I had reoccurring visions of my father taking a silver envelope from some unknown person. I had the vision three nights in a row. By this time, my mom had given her life to Christ. She attended church regularly. I explained what I saw, and she didn't know what to tell me. We went to a revival; the evangelist didn't know either but instructed my mom to pray. We soon realized my daddy had a drug addiction. What is it Whitney Houston said about crack? "Crack is whack; it might be whack but it sure will make you do something strange to get that eight ball." My father had a running tab with the crack man/woman he worked with at a factory. They knew in two weeks they would get their money. He didn't steal from the family or anything like that; he just did his crack.

You may think well, okay, he became a crackhead; time does not permit me to tell of all the multiple times we went to rehab for alcohol or abuse of some kind. He wasn't a bad person overnight; my sisters and I adored him until we lost respect for him. He was our superhero, our protection from things that go bump in the night in addition to the thugs in the neighborhood. How could you embarrass us like that? How could you go from being a pillar of the community to being a crackhead?

He left my mom several times and moved in with various women in the same housing projects. Sometimes he and his new girlfriends would run out of food. My mom gave them a plate every time. This was one of the most difficult times of my life. Regardless of the reason why my daddy came to the house, I would not open the door. In fact, I called the police. He moved away since there wasn't a reason for him to be there.

I called my mom. I explained he was trying to kick the door in. I begged her to come home. She returned before the police responded; go figure. He came into the house with her. He charged at me; I was so afraid. I thought he would hit me like he hit her. What they didn't know is I had a knife; I didn't want to kill my father, so I jumped out the window.

This craziness went on for over 25 years, but by this time I was active in my church. I prayed and prayed for my dad to give up drugs. My prayers went unanswered for so long, I stopped praying. I felt that God didn't hear me. My parents got back together, and then the bottom fell out once more.

The day my mother was released from the hospital (she has battled some unknown disorder since 1999), I went by the house to visit. She was lying in bed unable to get something to eat or go to the bathroom. I told her this is enough; I am taking her with me. She was gone for a month before he realized she was gone for good. I thought this would make him get help; it didn't.

I had never seen my daddy this low, so I asked him one day, "Are you tired of this life?" He replied, "Yes." I asked, "Are you ready for help?" He simply said, "No." God has a way of working things out. By this time, the electric company had removed all the wires from the house. They cut it off; he would pay someone to cut it back on. Did I mention the water was off, and the house was completely inhabitable? There is a popular television series where they say, "Winter is coming." Well, it came with a vengeance.

It was so bad (20 below zero) the crack man was calling me to let my dad live with me. I will not go into detail about that conversation. Please know I didn't cuss; I kept it classy because I am a lady. When I finally reached my dad, these were my exact words: "You cannot live with me; I will take you for treatment. This is your only option." He agreed to go; thank God.

Not to belabor my portion of this book... after treatment, my dad realized it wasn't enough. He chose to stay in Howell, Michigan to attend additional treatment as well as to be close to his sponsor. Who was this person? My family and I were so impressed by this slow transformation. When he completed treatment, he made Howell his home for him and my mom.

Where is the beauty of this story? He regained the respect of his family. We were allowed to get five years of the person we once knew: a loving caring father, grandfather, husband and brother. Years ago, in the midst of his drug addiction, I remember God telling me I would have to take care of my father; I boldly told God I would not. As my father recovered from drug and alcohol abuse, he developed prostate cancer.

Every morning after coming home from working the midnight shift, I dressed my mother for the day, fixed her breakfast, and then took my father to treatment for eight weeks. Not one day did I complain; it was an honor. While in nursing school, he had to have hip replacement surgery. I was there every day. I had taking care for my parents down to a science; both my parents were in the rehabilitation center at the time. I washed his clothes on Wednesday and hers on Saturday and prepared a home cooked meal every Sunday for them both.

I know my dad told me he loved me, but I really don't remember a time or the place. What I do remember is him telling me he was proud of me. That means more to me than anything in the world. How do I tie in the aftermath of his death? You have a 19-year-old young man who literally makes a conscious decision to place his name in the box marked father on the birth certificate, knowing full well that is not his biological child. You take that same man who raises that child as his own with all the perks and benefits of his biological children. Then leaves everything to her. That her is me.

You see, my daddy died suddenly without warning. Literally, I was talking to him on the phone when he complained of chest pain. I told him to call 911. As I rushed to get to his home, I called to check on the situation only to be told, "The coroner is on the way." Wait. What? The who is on the way where? I broke down while driving on the expressway; tears flowed so heavily, I could not see the road. I contemplated crashing my car, or driving into a body of water never to be found. My mother did not raise any punks, so I put my big girl panties on and did what I had to do.

I was tasked with planning the funeral, packing up my parents' home, and moving my mother with me while maintaining a brand-new startup job. Who had time to grieve? I had things to do with very little time to do them in. You would think I would have help but, conveniently, everyone else had plans. One of my village told me, "You should have told me sooner; I have a life; I have plans." *Excuse the hell out of me; I didn't plan on my daddy dying last week,* as my eyes lifted to this person looking at them with a blank stare.

After the funeral, my mom received calls for TVs, furniture, money. I sent a general text explaining although my dad is dead, my mother is not. She will be watching the 64-inch TV; she will be sitting on her sofa, and all the money was left in my name because he knew she would give it all to you. Keep in mind he had a nice jewelry collection he wanted to be distributed to the family, which I had no problem doing. Somewhere along the way, things became different and distant with my otherwise close family.

The plans for holidays fell to the wayside and were replaced by reason that we would not have our traditional gatherings on Memorial Day, Fourth of July, and Labor Day. As Thanksgiving approached, I saw my family pulling away from each other. Oh, the horror. I could see the closeness that my family shared slowly dissipating like the cold winter snow, as I saw the destruction of my family. I remembered I'd postponed my daddy's surprise birthday party to my daily regret; I thought I had more time to share life experiences with him, laugh with him, just to love him. I. Thought. I. Had. More. Time!

Realizing that time is so short, I fought to keep my family together. Instead of just hosting my One Annual Dinner on New Year's Day, I prepared a dinner for Thanksgiving and Christmas and welcomed everyone into my home. I thought we had turned a corner when my mom brought up my daddy's death; she sadly said one of my sisters was still very upset. I became agitated because I thought it was about the stuff. I was very short with my mom; I asked her what the problem was. She said, "They are upset because you still have your biological father, and they do not." I can still see my biological father, the man that has never been there for me, but they could not see their dad. According to my mom, I was referred to as a stepdaughter. Shut the front door (for lack of a great curse word). After fifty-two years, I have been regulated to a stepsister (no disrespect to step kids around the world). Those words hurt as if a dull dagger was shoved through my heart twice. Okay, I know you are confused; my dad was not my biological father. He was the man who stepped up to the plate to care for a child that was not his, but loved me unconditionally like his own birth daughter. My mother started dating my dad while pregnant with me.

He was the only man I know as a dad. He was my dad in every aspect of the word, and I carried his last name. Never one day did I feel unloved or less than my sisters. How was I supposed to react to this knowledge? At first, I was angry. I thought to myself, *Damn, baby, tell me how you really feel.*

I wanted to hurt them back. I spoke to my good friend Liz; I shared what my mom told me. She asked me how I felt. My response was simple, "How horrible a birth daughter were they that their father would leave his possessions to a stepdaughter?" Liz calmly replied, "You know you can't say that." She went on to explain, "You all are hurting. You are doing it separately, which is making it worse. You need to come together for a resolution."

God always has a plan for our good. I received a call from my aunt, and she said my sisters wanted to have a meeting about my dad's death. We met at my home; my middle sister claimed she didn't get anything. Stuff; we are meeting about stuff. They could have had all that curse word stuff if I could have had him back. I reminded my sister, "You don't remember getting freezers, dishes, towels, and various other things? You don't remember getting your driver's responsibility paid and reinstatement fees paid?" She couldn't look me in my face.

My other sister pulled out a curse word list with ought's against my mom. What the hell?! What you are not going to do is attack my mother because of your hurt and pain. Nope; not today. The world didn't revolve around you then or now. One by one, each complaint I shot it down. Her final complaint, "I didn't get any of my fathers' stuff." Cool baby-girl. I have a basement full of his stuff. Take your pick; it is still down there. I gave her the jewelry; I told her she could be responsible for getting it to the intended parties.

I was hurt beyond belief; I thought my family was better than stuff, better than TVs, sofas, cars, and other various things. I thought we loved each other more than material possessions, as one of my nephews said, "I just want my inheritance." I thought we were better than inheritance. I thanked them for showing me who we really were. Do I love them any less? Absolutely not; I love them all the more.

My dad leaving me all the money created so much drama. He knew no matter what, I would use that money to take care of my mother, when he could not help himself. I was there, no matter how low he went. After this, I saw the ugly side of us; we are not much different than many other families. I have made a conscious decision to love past it. I could have spoken out in anger, causing irreparable damage. I chose to love in spite of it. I will never tell them I know I was referred to as a stepsister. I love my family, and I have no problem telling them how I feel. I love you, forever and always.

Curtain Call: People often say, those that have died come back to visit. I know that happened to me. Prior to completing my portion of the book, I was scheduled to go out of town. I wanted to take my dad's camera, but I didn't know where it was. We also lost the cord when I moved my mom from Howell. I just so happened to look on the floor in front of my closet, and there was the camera laying on the floor. I quickly picked it up, then I thought *I still don't have the cord*. As I looked at the camera, I believed I had another plug that would work. I tried to put the alternate cord in that section. For some reason it wouldn't fit. I stuck my hand down into the compartment and, low and behold, the original camera cord. As tears streamed down my face, I silently said, "Thank you, Daddy! I love and miss you."

Collateral Beauty

Death is something we rarely talk about to express our final wishes. Death can bring about the ugly side of people. Sonya took the higher road and decided to hold her family together. How do you love past the hurts someone has caused you?

Chapter 5
Faith that Restores
by Sherry L. Peak

The most beautiful flowers are often given in the form of people; mothers in particular. Mothers are so loving and so kind. At least that is what comes to mind when I think about my mother. Ever since I can remember, my mother was always there helping me, loving me, and supporting me in everything I did.

No matter what was going on, she was there through the good, the bad, and the ugly. When I made mistakes, she told me it would be okay when I fell. She helped me get back up, and when I wanted to quit, she pushed me to keep going. She was my biggest fan; that one cheerleader who never missed her cue rooting for me whether near or far. She was a woman of great faith, my personal prayer warrior, my natural and spiritual mother, my friend, my confidant; she was my mama.

But what do you do when your heart has been broken into a million little pieces and your cheerleader, the one who is usually there to help you pick up the pieces and put them back together, is no longer there? Sometimes life happens, and it happens fast; without any warning, without any notification, and without any time to prepare. Often in these moments, there is only a split second to make a decision that will affect you for the rest of your life. That is what happened to me on November 24, 2001. Life happened, and I was not prepared.

For years I have eagerly awaited the month of November to arrive because it is the start of the holiday season with Thanksgiving Day kicking off the festivities. It is the season where many reflect and express gratitude for the blessings in their lives. It is a time when we enjoy vacation days, family gatherings, good eating and, for some, Black Friday shopping. Thanksgiving 2001 was no different for me. As the Thanksgiving holiday season approached, I spent weeks leading up to Thanksgiving Day talking on the phone with Mama about the menu and assigning tasks to those coming to dinner. After much planning, we finally made our annual trip to the grocery store in hopes of finding much-anticipated sales on the items needed for dinner.

While shopping, I thought back on how from the time I was a little girl I had watched my mother selflessly love, support, and provide for her family with very few days off of work. She would decline taking personal, sick, and vacation days off work so that she could receive the pay and use that money to help her children, grandchildren, and other family members. See, mama was the type of mother who lived to see her family happy. She was a woman of modest means and few treasures, but she had a heart of gold and a love that could conquer anything!

As I got older and began having similar experiences as Mama, I realized the true meaning and value of the sacrifices she made in her tiredness and suffering. So I routinely looked for ways that I could help her lighten her load and taking the lead in planning the Thanksgiving Day dinner was an opportunity to do that. It was one way I could show my love and appreciation to the one person who had selflessly given of herself to me and others all year long. I was so excited on Thanksgiving Day because I had just purchased my first home (with the help of my mother), and I was hosting the family gathering! Mama was just as excited because now all she had to do was show up for the festivities. We had good food, played Uno, watched movies, and told stories that made everyone in the house laugh! We sang along as the music played on the CD player and danced with joy to every tune that hit the airwaves! A great time was had by all, just as we imagined! As the day came to an end, we cleaned up, put away the food, and began to prepare for the much anticipated Black Friday shopping weekend.

The following day, we woke up and headed to the stores with our shopping lists in tow to find all of the wonderful sale items we saw in the store ads. Some things we got, and some we didn't. But in any case, the thrill of shopping was the highlight of our day. After we finished shopping, Mama and I retreated to my home for leftovers and an afternoon of binge-watching P. Diddy's Making the Band. We watched this show for hours and hours; so much, that it started to get late in the evening, and all of the excitement from the last two days were beginning to catch up with us. Soon, our eyes began to drift shut, and we were fighting to stay awake, and it quickly turned from us watching TV to the TV watching us.

As 9:00 p.m. approached, Mama slowly began to fall asleep. As she drifted off to sleep, legs crossed and her head tossed back on the loveseat, I happened to glance over at her, and I can remember feeling an overwhelming sense of empathy for her because I knew she was tired and perhaps even exhausted. I felt sorry for her because I knew she needed to rest. In that same moment, my heart filled with adoration for her, and I had a childhood moment and desire to lay my head across her lap as she slept, but I didn't do it. I didn't do it because although it seemed like the perfect moment, it also seemed like it would be an awkward moment.

As the night grew darker, Mama awakened and headed home because she was always worried about being out late. As I walked her to her car, I also got into my car to visit my grandparents (my mother's parents), who lived just down the street. Once I arrived at my grandparent's home, I called Mama to check on her to make sure she had gotten home safely, and she had.

While I was visiting my grandparents, my grandmother wanted to have a Bible study about Joseph and his coat of many colors; although I really didn't want to, I settled in to appease her request. The story spoke of the many tests and trials that Joseph encountered throughout his lifetime and how he relied on his faith to get through them. Although I had heard this story on several occasions, for some reason as I listened that night, I became engrossed in my thoughts as I reflected on how my strong faith had gotten me through the many tests and trials I had experienced in my life.

After the Bible study ended, I briefly talked to my grandparents and then decided to head home around 11:00 p.m. because I was exhausted. I hugged them and told them I loved them, and then gathered my belongings and headed to the door. As I approached the door and reached for the doorknob, out of nowhere, a loud voice said: "I will give you peace that surpasses all understanding."

Startled and confused, I quickly pulled my hand away from the doorknob and in bewilderment I immediately replied, "Huh?" as I stood there frozen and in a daze trying to make sense out of what had just happened, wondering why the voice had spoken to me, and what was it going to give me peace about. After a few seconds, I realized the voice I heard was the still small voice inside of me. I then hesitantly replied, "Okay," because I didn't know what the voice was referring to.

The next morning around 6:30 a.m., life happened fast for me. I was awakened by someone knocking very hard on my front door nonstop. At first, I didn't go to the door, thinking they would go away. After all, it was 6:30 a.m. on a Saturday. However, the longer I ignored the knock, the stronger the knock became as if someone was demanding my attention. When I got to the door, to my surprise, it was my neighbor telling me that I needed to go to the hospital because my mother had just been taken there. I was puzzled by what I was told because my mother and I had just spent most of the prior day and evening together, and she seemed to be doing fine. So I quickly said to him, "You must mean my grandmother who lives down the street," and he sternly replied, "No... Your mother!"

After he insisted on me getting dressed and going to the hospital, I immediately rushed back into the house to call my mother, but she did not answer. I then quickly woke my daughter, and as we were scurrying around getting dressed, I was also making phone calls to my siblings and my grandparents to see if anyone had talked to Mama, and no one had. It was at that moment that I became anxious.

Once dressed, I rushed out of the house to find my neighbor still standing at my front door as to ensure that I was going to the hospital as he insisted. On my way to the hospital, I thought I would first drive to Mama's house. When I arrived, I firmly knocked on the door several times, but I didn't get an answer. Now, by this time, I was a nervous wreck and took off driving 90 mph to the hospital to see what was going on with my mother.

When I arrived at the hospital, I was greeted by a staff person who immediately escorted me into a small room where I nervously waited for someone to come and tell me how my mother was doing. My heart was racing a million miles a minute. I didn't know what to do or to think. I was all alone. As I sat waiting, I looked around at the items in the room as a means to try to figure out what was going on. The room had several chairs and a table that had books, magazines, and a phone sitting on it. Still confused and somewhat in a daze, my eyes roamed to the door where a gentleman in a dark suit entered the room. He greeted me and promptly began asking me questions: What was my name? What was my mother's name? Had my mother been ill? When was the last time I saw my mother? Was I at the hospital alone?

After a few minutes of the questioning, I began to feel overwhelmed and began frantically asking what was going on with my mother. The gentleman encouraged me to remain calm as he continued to ask questions. I was growing weary and afraid, but I obliged him by answering a few more questions. When he was done, I demanded to know how my mother was doing. It was then that the still small voice inside of me spoke again saying, "Pay attention," as if it was preparing me for something, so I began to look around the room a second time, and as my eyes scanned the room, it was as if the light had been turned on.

While looking a second time, I noticed the room that I was sitting in was actually a small chapel filled with Bibles, Christian magazines, Kleenex, and holy crosses. As I continued to look around, my eyes landed on the nametag of the gentleman in the dark suit. The badge identified him as the chaplain. Still unsure as to why the chaplain was talking to me, I slowly looked up from his nametag as I asked again how my mother was doing. When our eyes locked, I could see that he was troubled. As I waited for an answer there was a brief moment of silence, and with dismay he said, "Ma'am, I am sorry, but your mother has passed away."

I was so not expecting to hear that news! I went into a state of total shock, so much so that as soon as the chaplain finished his sentence, I simultaneously threw myself back in the chair that I was sitting in, and I literally felt my mind snap. Snap into a million little pieces from pure shock and information overload that had short-circuited my mind. At that very moment, that still small voice said to me again, "Sit up and pay attention," as if it was calming me while also serving as a buffer between sanity and insanity. I then sat back up in the chair, took a few deep breaths, and said to the chaplain, "I think I should go check to see if my family has arrived."

As I left the chapel and walked down the hallway, I found a quiet corner and began to weep. I was utterly devastated. I could not wrap my mind around what I was just told. My entire body was trying to shut down, and I got sick to my stomach; repulsed at the news as I thought about how there would be no more talks with Mama, no more hugs, no more chances to lay my head in her lap, how much I still needed her, how much I was going to miss her, and how my life would never be the same without her.

While I was standing there, the same voice that spoke to me the night before spoke again saying, "I will give you peace that surpasses all understanding." When I heard those words a second time, now in the face of death, I then understood the relevance of the Bible study and the still small voice that spoke to me the night before. It was then that I felt an overwhelming sense of comfort that assured me that I was not alone, and everything would be alright.

The reassurance of the still small voice gave me the strength to make the decision not to give in to the mental snap of losing my mother, but rather to fight for my mind and well-being like I know my mother would have wanted me to do. So after spending a few minutes alone, I composed myself and walked to the waiting room, and as my family arrived one by one, I told them the news that Mama had passed away.

The road to healing in the days, months, and years that followed was difficult, but like Joseph, I relied on my faith to get me through the most difficult test I had ever faced. A test that was meant to break me, but it was God's peace and Mama's memory that graciously kept me safe. Now, I can stand in the face of adversity as a woman of strength, hope, and faith that my mother raised me to be.

As a part of my healing journey, I focused on practicing the following principles to strengthen and restore myself spiritually, mentally, and emotionally:

- Invite God into your situation;

- Permit yourself to live;

- Pray that God will lead and guide you through your time of transition;

- Learn to trust and follow the still small voice within;

- Give yourself time and space to grieve;

- Do the necessary work to heal;

- Find a safe space to share your thoughts and emotions;

- Stay connected to family, friends, and spiritual mentors;

- Remain active in your daily activities; and,

- Live each day to the fullest

Practicing these principles regularly helped me move from a place of pain to a place of peace and brighter days. So, if you are having a difficult time with the loss of a loved one, I invite you to consider practicing these principles, so that you too can see brighter days!

Dedicated to the life, legacy, and memory of Yvonne W. Peak

Collateral Beauty

Sherri faced the sudden death of her mother, but God had already laid the foundation and put the supports in place. She felt as if the still small voice gave her the fortitude to guard her mind. If you have faced an unexpected death, upon reflecting back do you see how God's hand was present?

Chapter 6
Chosen and Changed
by Felicia Wilkerson

Many people will walk in and out of your life, but only true friends will leave footprints in your heart.
Eleanor Roosevelt

It is such an honor and a blessing to be chosen. We've heard it said friends are extra special because we choose them to be in our lives. I had the awesome privilege of being chosen by two extraordinary ladies who have left footprints in my heart and from which I have learned great life lessons. When they passed away, the grief was unbearable. I give honor, love, and gratitude to these two wonderful women, Revodia Poindexter Johnson and Nedra LaShun Hardin.

Revodia Poindexter Johnson

I met Ms. Johnson when I was 13 years old. It was the end of my 8th grade school year, and I was "given" to her by my 8th-grade computer teacher, Mrs. Maria Shelton. I knew there was something special about her when Mrs. Shelton introduced us. She was a lovely woman, lean, well-dressed with a blazer and belt, salt and pepper hair wearing a beret, and a deep, majestic voice that demanded attention. She had a wide, beautiful smile, and I was pleased she was smiling at me. I trusted Mrs. Shelton and considered her a school mom. She'd shown me some adults could still be trusted and who kept their word. I knew if she said Ms. Johnson was trustworthy, it had to be true.

Mrs. Shelton had already made a significant impact on my life by keeping it 100 with me, keeping her word, and showing me love and support without my having to work for it. She showed me what my great, great, great grandmother showed me, unconditional love. Unbeknownst to me, Ms. Johnson would show me this same love for 28 years, until the day she left this earth.

The day I met Ms. Johnson, my life was changed. Mrs. Shelton explained to me that Ms. Johnson was the Home School Coordinator at Dunbar High School, and she would look after me and ensure I had what I needed to stay in school. For some reason, I trusted her, and I opened my heart and mind to her. That was one of the most significant decisions of my life because she showed me and taught me another way of being. Since I was only 13 years old, I was able to glean from her wisdom, knowledge, and a different perspective I may not have gotten otherwise. Not only did Ms. Johnson keep her word to Mrs. Shelton, but more importantly, she kept her commitment to God concerning me. She was an integral part of me getting through my young adult life. Ms. Johnson was with me through all of my highest and lowest moments in life. She was my soft place to land, my pillar of strength and wisdom.

Have you ever had people in your life who had high expectations of you? Did these people inspire you to ride on their faith and expectation until you believed in yourself? That's what Ms. Johnson [and Mrs. Shelton] did for me. She did ensure I graduated from high school and did so early.

Because of my living conditions as a child on her own, I was a teen parent at the age of 16. But you know what? She didn't throw me away or judge me. She did what a loving mother would do. She gave me Godly counsel, made sure I got medical care, made sure I ate vegetables and took my vitamins, and taught me how to care for a baby. She never made me feel like I was less than anyone else. Sure, she wanted to prevent me from getting pregnant, but once it was too late, she loved me through it. She paid for me to go to summer school, so I could get finished with high school quicker. On graduation day, no one from my blood family was there, but she was at the bottom step with a bouquet of flowers waiting for me to cross the stage. When I saw her, my heart smiled, and my eyes filled with tears. This was true love, a mother's love, and I was so very blessed to have her.

She would always introduce me by saying, "This is my daughter [or my child] that God gave me." I smiled every time she said it, but it wasn't until she was gone that I received complete revelation knowledge that God purposed her to be my mother's love.

You see, at the time, my birth mother didn't know how to love us because she didn't love herself, and you can't expect people to give you what they don't have. And Mother Johnson proudly became my mom and my children's grandma. Tell me, how can one lady be available for births of your children, at school and college graduations, and available for counseling whenever needed? What lady can hear from God, call you, and tell you the Spirit told her to tell you something, and it was always an on-time word? Ms. Johnson, that's who—my mother's love. And, the thing that took me most by surprise was, at her funeral she was just that to so many other people. I still weep over her not being here because for some reason I thought I'd always have her. She'd been my biggest and best cheerleader and teacher for so long; I never imagined life without her. I could write an entire book about everything Ms. Johnson did for me, our conversations and time spent together. But what I can surely say is that she was a Godsend and my very own personal angel.

I hadn't talked to Momma Johnson since she moved to Houston to live with her daughter, Leonora. I wanted to speak to her so badly. I missed our heart-to-heart conversations, and I loved to hear and glean from her wisdom and hear her say, "Chile, the spirit..." In retrospect I wish I would have done more to reach out to Leonora and her granddaughter, Shellsia, to speak to her. I still loved her, and I know she still loved me.

The day I received the news that she had passed away, it felt as if my heart fell into the pit of my stomach. I couldn't believe it, even though she was 84 years old; I just couldn't believe it. Immediately my mind recalled all of the years we'd spent together, and I wept over my missed opportunities. At her funeral, I wept sorely at her casket saying, "Thank you, thank you, thank you." I know she knew how very grateful I was for her, but I just couldn't thank her enough.

You see, people don't have to love you as deeply as she loved me. She truly fulfilled God's calling to love the "little ones." Thank you, Ms. Revodia Poindexter Johnson. I love you very much, and my heart is full of love and gratitude for you. Thank you for being a mentor, counselor, friend, and mother. Thank you for your guidance, your care, and your love. I will never, ever forget you.

"Iron sharpeneth iron; so a man sharpeneth the countenance of his friend."
(Proverbs 27:19)

Nedra LeShun Hardin

I met Nedra Hardin at church. She joined the church and then the sanctuary choir. She had a wonderful sense of humor, loved to laugh, and loved music just like me. One night at choir rehearsal, after having a hilarious time together, I asked her if she wanted to be friends. She smiled and responded enthusiastically, "Yes!" That was the beginning of a beautiful friendship. It was actually the first friendship I initiated in my adult life. All my other friendships stemmed from childhood, or during a traumatic time in my life. I didn't and still don't have very many friends, so her acceptance of my friendship was special. For some reason, she was so in awe of me asking her to be friends.

Our friendship blossomed. We talked on the phone all the time. For a couple of years, I worked third shift at a call center, and Nedra would call me, and we'd talk about everything. She told me about her time spent in the military, how she "used to" be and what God delivered her from. She'd talk lovingly about her mom, dad, and sisters. She shared her secrets and her heart.

Nedra was the type of person who made you feel very comfortable. She was so transparent with her experiences and feelings, you couldn't help but open up to her. So, I did it. I let her in and shared my heart and life with her. I told her my life story, as she did, and our bond grew closer.

She spent a lot of time over the years with my family at my home, and my kids affectionately called her Sister Nedra.

We sang, laughed, cried, and prayed together. I recruited Nedra to feed the homeless with me for my outreach ministry, and she was absolutely honored and glad to do it. But at one point in our relationship, I talked with Nedra because I felt like she loved me too much. It hurt her, and that was not my intention. But I couldn't understand how she could love a friend to that degree, purely and sister-like. She truly loved being my friend. I did not have a revelation on God's purpose for her.

Nedra wasn't married and didn't have any children, but she had a slew of people whom she loved and who loved her and called her friend. Her assignment was to teach us what pure and true friendship looked like and how it felt. Only, I seemed to only be able to receive so much of it; major mistake. I regret I hurt her feelings. But we repaired our friendship, though it wasn't quite the same, and we were friends for 15 years before she died of breast cancer.

I'll never forget the day she told me she had stage four breast cancer. She held my hand when she told me. I responded, "So what does that mean?" She whispered, "Stage five is in the grave." We wept. We had a big birthday celebration for her 40th birthday shortly after her mastectomy. All of her family and closest friends were there and, in true Nedra style, there was lots of singing. We serenaded her. Even though she didn't feel well and was having a hard time breathing, she hung in there for us.

About a month and a half before she passed away, she was in the V.A. hospital in Dallas. I went for a visit and ended up staying until 3 a.m. In between her violent vomiting, we talked at times, and other times we sat in silence. I remember around midnight, I told her to scoot over, and I got in her hospital bed with her. She lay her head on my shoulder and quietly wept. She knew she was dying, and that can be kind of scary even if you're saved. She was strong, though, and even from her hospital bed, she was still loving and giving advice. Even though Nedra was a few years younger than I was, I always enjoyed her company, and she had an old soul.

The next month, Nedra went into the hospital and never came out. My biggest regret was not keeping my phone charged because I missed the call from her sister, Carla, to come to the hospital and be with the family when she was taking her final breaths. When I received the word of her passing from Crystal, a mutual church friend, I was devastated. Gone. Just like that. Not even seven months earlier, we'd had a girl's day out and were hanging out at Sundance Square, and just like that she was gone.

Nedra's absence has left a void in my life, and it was then that I realized—just like with Ms. Johnson—her friendship was God-ordained. We've heard the saying people are brought into your life for either a reason or a season, and this was definitely true of Nedra. She was truly one of a kind, and I miss her immensely. I'm grateful for 14 years of friendship and sisterhood.

Collateral Beauty

Grief has a way of making you reflect. As I reflect on the lives of these two ladies and their impact on me, I am humbled. I used to grieve over what I never had, and now I've had the chance to grieve over what I had and lost. But now I realize, even though they are not physically present with me, what they gave me... love, friendship, and a sense of belonging... can never be diminished. If I knew then, what I know now, I would have cherished the time spent together even more. I would have told them I love them more. I would have told them thank you more.

My heart's prayer: Lord, help me to redeem the time. Help me to honor relationships. I miss my friend, Nedra, so much, and I wish I'd put more into our friendship in the latter years. She taught me the meaning of true friendship. That was her purpose: to show us what true "brotherly love" looks like. She was unselfish, loved at all times, was giving, caring, and considerate. How blessed I am to have had someone love me like that! So Father, in my remaining relationships, help me to honor them and appreciate them! Help me not to take their presence for granted. The same goes for Mama Johnson. She was my mother's love. Oh, how I miss her and love her and need her Godly counsel. I didn't know she was my mother's love until she left me. Help me, Lord, to be ever mindful of my relationships—what people are to me and who/ what I am to others. Help me, Lord. Renew, restore, and revive my relationships. Help me to be to someone who these ladies were to me. I want to be someone's special person. In Jesus' name. Amen.

"A friend loveth at all times..."
Proverbs 17:17 NIV

Chapter 7
Finding Joy in the Journey
by Joy Jones-Reed

The journey was rough! Mighty, mighty rough!

Have you ever felt like God was so far away that even your deepest prayer could not reach Him? Have you ever felt that your faith was so strong, and within the blink of an eye, it seemed as if it just vanished into thin air? Having been in church all my life and feeling a strong connection with God, when the unexpected came knocking at my door, I felt all of those things and more. Now, walk with me as I travel down a dark path of uncertainties that transpired in my life.

It all started in 2006 when I received the news that my husband and I were expecting twins. Oh, the *joy*! Little did we know that blissful moment would ultimately turn into something we totally weren't expecting. The twins were born premature, weighing only 1lb and a few ounces each. I was only 24 weeks when they made their grand entrance into the world. It seemed as if it was all so surreal. They both had a 60%-70% chance of *not* surviving. Our daughter had several blood transfusions, and our son had a total of five surgeries on his tiny little body, including a gastrointestinal surgery due to a blockage.

They both stayed in the NICU for nearly 100 days. Those were days of worry, days of hurt, days of being confused as to why this happened, and days of traveling to two different hospitals because they had to be separated due to their many complications. As a parent, it's hard watching your children fight for their lives, and there is nothing you can do to help them. Thanks be to God, they both came home healthy and without any machines.

During the latter part of that same year, my mother suffered a massive stroke. Talk about an unexpected blow that I did not see coming! I quickly rushed to Memphis where my mother resided. She was in ICU for months. It seemed as if she was not going to pull through this. Now, what was I to do? I had premature twins at home that required my attention and a mother who was on life support fighting for her life happening all at the same time. Where is God? Where is that strong faith I proclaimed to have? I was crumbling. I did not know if I was going or coming. I was perplexed and dismayed. Then, as the years passed by, things started looking up. The twins grew into beautiful, healthy children, and my mother was doing a lot better despite her condition. Even though there were some hardships along the way, I felt as if there was still hope and life could still be sweet again.

In 2016, life hit hard. I received a call on January 29th that my mother was unresponsive and had to be placed on life support once again. It was like the cycle was repeating itself from the very first time the stroke happened. But this time I knew it was different. I knew deep down that she wouldn't pull through. There were no words to describe how I knew; I just felt it in my spirit. Everything came rushing to me at once, as I expeditiously made my way to Memphis once again to be by her side. All the memories, all the sleepless nights worrying about my mother, all the heartaches and wishing there was more I could have done, even all the prayers I have ever prayed on her behalf... it all came crashing down on me.

When I arrived at the hospital and saw my mother, the doctors informed me that her condition was not getting any better because her lungs were failing. There were times when she was alert, and doctors thought they could wean her off the ventilator to see if she was able to tolerate it. Every time they tried to lower the vent, she could not take it. Her body was too weak to breathe on her own. Even though this was happening, my mother would still recognize people and be alert enough to understand conversations (because she couldn't talk) and even smile and grin every now and again. It makes you wonder how a person who was suffering from respiratory failure, who was hooked up to life support, and whose body was too weak to do anything could be so alert.

I shall never forget when the doctor told me that a decision had to be made about removing her from life support. At that point, I looked at the doctor with a deep look of concern and said, "Look, doctor, I need you to give it to me straight. No sugar coating, no beating around the bush. Is there a chance that she could pull through this?" He responded by saying, "At this point, chances are very slim that could happen."

I recall the moments of walking up and down the corridor—nervous, frantic, confused, but most of all scared to death! My mind was racing. How was I going to break this news to my family? I didn't have the answers, but I knew I had to call them and deliver the devasting news. The family and I made the toughest decision we could have ever made, and that was to remove her from life support. My Lord! We need You, now! On February 14, 2016, at 12:15 a.m., on a Sunday morning (Valentine's Day), my mother went home... to her *heavenly home*.

But wait... that's not how the story ends...

I'll always remember how concerned my dad was about me when my mother passed. He knew I had a lot to deal with, so he made sure his baby girl was eating to keep my strength up. He would often tell me he was proud of the way I took care of my mother, and that I was a strong woman. He was one of my most significant supports during this heartbreaking moment in my life.

When I returned home to Dallas, the grief of losing my mother began to sink in, and I knew I would need to seek counseling. Let me tell you though... it works! Counseling is not designed to take the hurt and pain away, but it is designed to help you understand why you go through certain emotional and physical changes.

Before I could even set an appointment for counseling, I received yet another tragic phone call. This time concerning my dad. He was involved in a horrific car accident and was paralyzed from the shoulders down. All of this took place just two weeks after I buried my mother. So, again, I hurried back to Memphis only to receive news that my dad's organs were shutting down, and he would have to be removed from life support.

My dad passed away on March 5, 2016, at 1:15 a.m., on a Saturday. I was in total shock. Devastated! I was numb. I just lost my mother and now my dad less than three weeks later. God, this can't be happening. I was living in a total nightmare. I was very close to both of my parents, and there were no words to describe the pain I was feeling from this double loss.

When I returned home to Dallas from my dad's burial, I was still in a state of shock. It just didn't seem real. I was emotionless. Anxiety began to creep within the depts of my soul. Air would begin to escape my body. Sleep and I were like distant cousins. I didn't know what to think or do. I was in such a state of shock that for months and months, I couldn't even *pray*. I did not have enough strength to muster up the words to even begin to talk to God. At this point, my body was going through all sorts of changes both physically and emotionally. My hair began to fall out; my skin broke out in a rash, and my weight fluctuated. I was completely *grief stricken*.

During the year, the Lord spoke to me and said: "*Trust Me.*" He knew the plans He had for my life. *He* wanted me to lean and depend on *Him*. He also knew that this wasn't the end of the story. In 2017, the unexpected came knocking at our door again. Remember those beautiful, healthy, premature twins I mentioned earlier? Well, after taking my daughter to the doctor several times because of sinus issues, it was determined she would need surgery... and soon.

Just two weeks after her surgical procedure, my son became ill and had to have emergency surgery. It was determined that he was suffering from Acute Bowel Obstruction. This meant his intestines were twisted. The doctor told us chances were very high that they would have to remove part of his intestines, and he would more than likely have to have a colostomy bag for the rest of his life. He was only 10 years old.

After losing my parents the year before, my daughter having unexpected surgery, and now this devastating news about my son, *where is my faith*? I'll tell you exactly where it is... It is within me, and I had to pull it out. It was Tony Evans who once said that when disaster strikes, be encouraged in *His* ability to meet you right where you are.

Let me tell you, the Lord met me. He met me when He told me to trust Him. He met me when He called both my parents home to be with Him. He met me when my children had to have serious unexpected surgeries. He met me during those sleepless nights. He met me when I could not breathe, and anxiety set in. He met me when I was perplexed and numb. He met me when I would cry behind closed doors until there were no more tears left to cry. Yes, *He met me!* And He will meet you, too.

I decided to trust God and to activate my faith. Come here faith... the twins both recovered from their surgeries just fine. Faith... when our son came out of his three-hour operation, the doctor came and told us that they *did not* have to remove any of his intestines, and he would never need a colostomy bag. What a mighty God we serve! I went through all of that, plus the fact that I was still grieving the death of my parents. Oh! Did I mention I was in the process of still recovering from a back surgery that I'd had before the passing of my parents? Yep!

You have to realize that God uses suffering for good. You may be saying to yourself; how can one even establish the fact that good can come out of your loved one's death or that terrible unexpected situation? Here is how: He can take and restore unto you the joy of your salvation. God will begin to help you understand that there is a broader view; a greater story of love and our lives on earth doesn't compare to the glorious eternity that is spent with Him. That's the bigger picture!

I told you that God kept telling me to trust Him. He wants you to trust Him, too. I'm reminded of when God told me to go out and inspire others. I said, "Okay, Lord, but I don't know how I am going to do that. I'm still broken and going through the grief process myself." Afterwards, everything became still. It was like God was silent. Then all of a sudden, God woke me up in the middle of the night and told me, "The race is not given to the swift nor the battle to the strong." And as the tears flowed, I could still hear Him saying, "I have equipped you. Keep running the race." That is what I want to say to you... *Keep running the race!*

Keep running the race! Keep running to the One who is able to see you through. Keep fighting and pressing your way. There is a more significant work within you. There is a purpose behind all of your pain. Know that God is your strong tower. He is your power source when life's unexpected circumstances knock the living wind out of you. Be on your guard; stand firm in faith; be courageous, be strong. (1 Cor 16:13)

The Lord said, "My Grace is sufficient for you; for my power is made perfect in weakness." Learn to enjoy the simple pleasures of life by finding joy in the journey. There is nothing wrong with being stuck in grief because when you love deeply, you grieve deeply. Just don't stay there. When you are having a good day, enjoy it. Do what brings happiness to your life, and do not feel guilty for doing so. Lean into your grief, and do not run from it. Trust the grief process even when you can't understand it. When those emotions swell within you out of the blue, and the tears begin to stream down, allow it to happen. Tears cleanse the soul. Never feel that you have to be on anyone else's time as to how long it should take you to grieve. Grieving is a process, not a time frame. It could take weeks, months, or even years.

One thing that I have learned is that time doesn't heal all wounds; God does. You will eventually get to a place where you can learn to embrace the "new normal" of your life—a place where you can talk about your loved one and smile at all the beautiful memories they left behind. When you get to that place, you can look around and see the amazing wondrous works of God. The sun will then shine upon your face, and you will know that He gave you beauty for your ashes.

The collateral beauty of it all is that no matter how bad the situation is, that's not the result. You can either allow your circumstances to make you bitter, or they can make you better. I chose to allow it to make me better. So, continue to *go in faith*. How beautiful it is when you can look back and say *if it had not been for the Lord on my side...*

My prayer:

Lord, I sure do thank you for giving me faith through the storms of life. I thank you that I can once again find Joy in the Journey; the Joy that only You could provide. I pray now that my words have inspired everyone who reads this book. Be a source of peace to those who are brokenhearted. I pray that You send your Comforter to be with them, and I pray they will know that there is still hope, despite the circumstance. You are God and God alone. All praises belong to You. Thank you for loving us and never leaving our side. This is my prayer. In Jesus' name, Amen.

"Now to Him who is able to do exceedingly abundantly above all that we ask or think, according to the power that works in us."
(Ephesians 3:20)

Chapter 8

Your Knight in Shining Armor May Just Be an Old Ghost

by Catalina Hernández

Life is made up of experiences, good and bad. Some experience is gained with little loss, while other experience can be quite costly. There are many lessons to be learned in marriage, and in my case, I learned what I had never seen anyone experience, much less expected to live out myself.

To begin with, I had been raised around some level of dysfunction. However, seeing that I had always been at the periphery of the unpredictability, as a sort of captive audience, I resented the circumstances of having to watch the instability and at seventeen decided to leave home early to disassociate myself from the madness altogether simply. However, the journey towards disassociation took much longer than I ever knew it would.

My threshold for dysfunction was almost innately higher than most people's. Because I had grown almost accustomed to emotional and verbal abuse, what others would register as red flags in their partners were merely flashing yellow lights that I made a mental note of, but never treated with real urgency. I was the youngest in my family and had always been expected to follow the rules of my elders. That meant having to submit to the rules of everybody around me at home. I had learned to make little noise when requests were made and to tolerate the antics of those older than myself.

As a child, I tried to make sense of these outbursts in the best light possible. I trusted that they were dealing with more responsibility and hardship than I could see, that they were protecting me from danger, and respected that they were more exposed to the difficulties of life than I was, clearly causing them to react in ways I never understood. This created in me an ability to please the people around me, seeing that I knew not to contribute to problems, but rather to make situations better by placating and removing myself from the situation before it could get any worse. With little knowledge of my own, I had become an ideal enabler.

I spent the duration of my marriage cleaning up my spouse's messes. I would hide his mistakes to protect him from criticism and complained little as to not contribute to the dissolution of the family. My motives were good and, as a woman of faith, I trusted that God knew what He was doing, and I learned to see my marriage as a test of faith, of will, and the jackpot was having a family.

After years of naively co-authoring our disaster, I began to see patterns emerge, a series of health issues arise in my young body, and the yellow lights become flashing red lights complete with barricades and railroad crossing gates. I stopped listening to the voice inside myself exclaiming for peace and began to demand it externally.

Despite my efforts of peace-making and cover-up, things got progressively worse. Approximately one year after our marriage, the man I once knew had done a total inverse, and another man emerged from my husband's shell. What was once accolades and tenderness had become criticism and blame. All of a sudden, he struggled with holding down a job, whereas before he worked long hours tirelessly, then paid the household bills and provided for our basic needs at home. Over a short amount of time, he began to give in to verbal attacks, emotional abuse, and failure to assume any financial responsibility whatsoever.

Three to five years into this behavior, his reactions began slipping into the realm of domestic violence with instances of snatching things out of my hands, having angry fits, even pulling my hair, and at one point flipping a table because his steak was not salted to taste. He had not hit me. I knew instinctively not to react to him, but after he calmed down, I would respond and sit down with him over coffee and be forthright about his behavior, fully informing him that I would not accept that kind of attack, warning him that it was destroying our marriage.

When I considered leaving, I would think, "This is the father of my child. What are my alternatives?" I was terrified of raising my son without a father. After all, I had a father, and if I had any intention of being a single mother, I would never have had a baby with my husband, right? Besides, I had made a promise to my husband, to myself and, most importantly, to God. My daily prayer was doing everything in my power to refuse, giving the enemy victory over my family. These words became my diet. I was dedicated to fasting, praying, getting on my knees, and asking daily for God's deliverance.

I refused to accept that emotional and verbal abuse was worthy of walking away. I had always associated divorce with a consumerist society that did not value people or humanity. I thought that divorce was like abandonment and having a "fast food" attitude of disposability towards family, and I wanted no part of it.

After years of this treatment, I found myself feeling helpless and desperate. Instead of my knight in shining armor respecting or valuing my ability to show discipline and self-restraint by communicating the need to talk through conflict to reach a solid solution, he began calling me pretentious and weak. Lastly, I suggested we seek counseling as a form of guidance and recourse. At the time, he denied counseling and was insistent that it was all in my head, or a reaction to something I was saying or doing at the time, and that he believed he was fully justified in his actions. If someone was to blame, it was me, he said.

I sought counseling alone, but because I did not see myself as the one with erratic or emotionally and physically violent behavior, I did not continue services. However, I did learn one important thing, and that was to stop blaming myself for this disaster because I could never have known this would happen. Or, did I? I began to do the heavy lifting of self-discovery and demanding more from my future. In that, I began to discover the learnings that had evaded me for so long. Many of my lessons had more to do with admitting the unthinkable than discovering the unknown. They looked something like this:

- **People may never tell you what they see in your partner if they think you are happy.**

The people around you love you. They know who you are and where you came from. They have seen you struggle through the ups and downs of relationships. They see your desire to do what is right and genuinely want what is best for you, and if they see you happy, then they may mute themselves if they see shady behavior from your partner. Doubt may appear subtly in the form of a question or an implied statement such as, "I didn't invite him because, well, I know he's always busy on Friday nights," or perhaps, "Why are you always alone on Friday nights? Where's your guy?" If at that point you provide a seemingly justified explanation, you do not appear to have a problem with it yourself; their concern may lessen considering that their boundaries and expectations of what they want for you may not match your expectations for yourself. Or, they decide to give you and your partner the benefit of the doubt. After all, they do not want to lose a friend over this.

- **We are creatures of habit. Your knight in shining armor may be an old ghost that you have yet to deal with.**

It is difficult to call the familiar strange. If we are raised in and around abusive situations, then we are likely going to repeat them. You can get as far away from them as you want, but if you have not faced the abuse and called it as such, the learning of this life lesson awaits you. Degrees and success do not absolve you from repeating these circumstances in your own life. The same dramas emerge but with new characters... new flavors; yet, the same themes play out. Pretending abuse was not there or running away from it dooms us to deal with it later, and marriage is the ideal place for this kind of learning. Seek counseling, read books, make elders who have survived difficulties your counselors and your friends. Try to avoid seeing yourself as an exception.

- **People will say or do whatever they think you want to get you to marry them.**

Many people are attracted to the idea of marriage. They are excited to see themselves in courtship and sharing their lives with a person a beautiful as you. They are attracted to your faith, your success, your kind spirit, and will want to align themselves with the light they see within you. This does not mean that they are any more prepared to treat you well and take care of you. They may or not be aware of their shortcomings, but if they think you are a special person and they may not find someone like you again, you can expect that they may resort to saying or doing anything to get you to commit to them. Their motives may be pure, and they may want someone to share their lives with, but difficult questions must be considered. Have they dealt entirely with their addictions? Have they accepted and healed from an abusive past? Have they outgrown their tendency to be unfaithful and deceptive? Do they possess poor financial habits, and if so, what have they done to better them? Good intentions do not ensure their preparedness for marriage.

This is forgoing the many suitors that have less than pure intentions and see you as a trophy, a financially smart decision, or an easy target. We must be aware and cautious about who we allow into our lives. Things are not always what they seem. Listen. People will reveal themselves to you if you simply listen and take them at their word.

- **Entrapment. It exists. Some people will use children as leverage to guilt you into staying in an abusive marriage, and it's not only women.**

It is not uncommon to hear men speak of women who try to trap them with children. It always saddened me to hear them talk this way about women because I had never seen us do anything like this. On the contrary, I have seen women use men, sometimes to give them a child, and then leave them, never so much as mentioning a pregnancy. However, in all my skepticism, I wonder if I was not targeted myself.

Once my son was born, my ex-husband did a transformation for the worst in every way imaginable. Being a woman of faith, he was sure that walking away was not going to be easy for me, and he all but set fire to every emotional, physical, and financial boundary I had set for myself and the marriage. He used my faith against me by praying and attending church with me, but never making an authentic effort to change.

Men know that nice women are hard to come by. They are aware that good mothers are also hard to come by. Add having a God-fearing heart to that mix, and you have one covetous woman! Abusive men know that if given a chance to have a child and start a family with a Proverbs 31 woman, means their wives are faithful and longsuffering and may likely tolerate more than they ever would have before having a family.

- **You don't know someone until you have married them.**

That said, many people wait for commitment before showing their true colors. This bears a dangerous resemblance to witchcraft, seeing that the desire to dominate, manipulate, intimidate, and control others is the root of sorcery. People see their desire to "hold back" or "hold out" their authentic self as a harmless attempt to gain the desired result. However, this lack of transparency is rooted in lies, manipulation, and the desire to control a situation to obtain a specific outcome. Unfortunately, it is very difficult to be aware of these changes in a person's personality before they manifest, and we may ignore the warning signs because of our affection for our partner and desire to believe the best in them during the time before the marriage. Frankly, once the marriage has occurred, it seems like it is already too late. Truth be told, it is never too late, and their efforts to control your life are only as effective as you allow them to be.

- **Don't be afraid of divorce – even God allowed divorce for particular circumstances.**

I am sure that God's design for marriage did not include one spouse destroying the other. I am also sure that marriage is not rooted in fear and manipulation. In fact, I am sure that marriage was created to be an earthly manifestation and demonstration of His love for us and was meant to be selfless, giving, and a submission to one another out of reverence for the other person's love and position in our lives and families. When we are naturally inspired by our spouse's affection and grace, we give love and mercy back out of a spirit of gratitude. This love is to be transparent and regenerative. This is not to say that we will not experience difficulties, but our complications should never enter the realm of abuse, adultery, or outright deception for selfish gain.

I have since left my marriage and have no regrets. There are things I would have changed, but given the limited knowledge I had at the time, I must forgive myself and accept that I did the best I could do at that season in my life. I wish I could say all of my relationships will be strictly and sharply perfect from here forward, but I have learned that by denying my faults, I will condemn myself to make the same mistakes yet again.

Today I see myself more clearly, and I see that I am broken, but I value myself more, and I fear much less than I ever did. Therefore, I am unafraid of life after the death of a relationship because I know that I am strong enough in myself and my faith to forgive myself for my imperfection, and have begun to demand from my partner the same kind of wellness, strength, and conscience I demand from myself without exception.

Chapter 9
LOCKED IN
by Ava Marie

I practiced for weeks. I thought about it constantly and rehearsed my speech. I prayed and cried and lamented over the decision. How will I tell him; what will I tell him? How will he respond? Should I say nothing and go while he's at work? What, when, and how am I going to do this?

After weeks of putting it off, I decided this is the day. We sat down to talk, and I said, "I'm leaving. I can't take the fighting, the cheating, the lies. I'm tired of it. I'm moving out!" A second after that came from my lips, I saw the fury rising in his eyes and felt the tension building in the room. He jumped up from his seat and slapped me in my face so hard, it knocked me out of my seat and down to the floor. He straddled my chest then put his knees on my hands. He was very loud, angry, and deliberate. He said, "No other man will have this face to look at! I will f**k you up. You won't be the same when you leave me!"

He started hitting me in my face with his fist. I couldn't cover my face to block the blows. I just turned from side to side, trying to lift my body and get him off me. I cried begging him to stop.

Tasting blood in my mouth from my teeth crashing into the inside of my cheeks, I started thinking, *he's gonna kill me.* "What's wrong? What did I do to you?" I yelled and pleaded with him. I tried to get loud enough to get past his furious assault and into a place where he could hear me and stop beating me, but to no avail. Anger had him; he was locked in.

I felt my eye swelling, and I can't explain it, but suddenly I felt physical strength come on me. I rolled myself hard enough to turn on my side and cover my face with the one free hand. He backed away while still saying that I wasn't ever leaving him. "You're bought and paid for," he shouted, as I ran into the bathroom and made sure I was locked in.

I looked around for anything I could use for a weapon if he forced his way into the bathroom. I grabbed the scissors and looked in the mirror. I looked at the knots forming on my head, and both my eyes were almost closed and swelling, my lip was split. My skin was red and hot in all the places it would be black and blue tomorrow.

I was afraid to go out of the bathroom for ice. I just knew he'd be standing right there. I decided to run cold water on towels and put that on my face. I was too scared to call the police. I thought he would be very angry and violent with me if they came to the house.

In my mind, I believed it wasn't his fault. It was my fault; I had made him so mad and provoked his wrath. He loves me; he says he loves me, but sometimes I make him so angry. He doesn't mean to hurt me.

My pulse was racing; mind on the go; get out of here forever... stay away; you keep making him mad. There is something wrong with you, Ava. You're gonna make him kill you.

The next couple of days were my days off. When it was time to go back to work, I called in sick. The sick policy at my job says on your third day off for sickness, you need a medical excuse to return. I didn't want to go to the doctor because I thought they would know what happened, and I was too embarrassed.

I went to work on the third day with so much makeup on, I looked like a corpse. The swelling in my lips had gone down because I kept ice on them. I could not cover the black eyes no matter what; they were still swollen. I bought some very dark sunglasses, put on a baseball cap, and went to work.

I worked at the main post office in Fort Worth, Texas. I was sitting at my sorter, doing my job when my supervisor approached me. He came next to me and asked if I had a prescription for the glasses. They were much darker than what was allowed on the work floor. I said, "No, they are not prescriptions, but I can't take them off." He said he couldn't let me wear them if they are not prescriptions; they were against dress code policy.

I repeated I couldn't take them off. The supervisor said, "I can't let you stay on the workroom floor. Come with me to the office, please, Mrs. James." I got up and followed him. When we walked into the office, he asked me why I had black glasses on and asked if I could even see through them. "Not good!" I said as I took the glasses off my face. He was shocked and exclaimed with deep empathy, "Oh, my God! What happened? Who did this to you?" Then, he just looked down at the floor and said, "Mrs. James, put the glasses back on, please. Are you alright? Do you need a doctor? Oh my God, I'm so sorry. You can't go back to work. You can't stay here like this. Can you see at all? What do you need?"

I told him I needed a week off, so I could find a place to live and get some things together. I was so ashamed and just kept my head down, as I began to weep in the office. He said he would send a female supervisor in to talk to me and bring the paperwork for my week off.

The next day I started secretly looking for a place to live. A safe place for me and my children. They were in

Michigan for a few weeks with my sister on summer break. I didn't want them to come home to this scene anymore.

I had left so many times before, and he always found the right combination of words to get me back home. But nothing ever changed after a while; he would be angry and punching me again about things that upset him and now, years later, I still don't know what the trigger for his violence was.

There was something different this time. I wasn't angry and emotional. I was tired of being treated that way. My mind was made up. I'm not taking anymore; I'm leaving for good. I didn't tell him that I was looking for a place.

The next week he was so full of I'm sorry's. He would say, "I'm sorry, but you make me so mad sometimes." I heard him, but I didn't hear him. His words fell on deaf ears.

He bought me a new diamond ring as a surprise one day. A few days later, he brought flowers home to me. None of the apologies or gifts mattered. I pretended to be impressed by them, so he wouldn't get mad. I continued to look for a place to move away, far away. I had heard too many apologies and suffered far too many battered and bruised days.

Finally, on that weekend I found the perfect place. It was a townhouse closer to work in a great neighborhood, and I gave them a deposit and filled out an application. Everything went through, and I was accepted as a new tenant. I was moving at the first of the month, and that was just two weeks away. Every day, I would take a couple of outfits from my closet and put them in my locker at work. I was happier than I'd been in years. I was so grateful and thanking God every few minutes.

The first of the month came, and I got the keys to my new place. I went there that night after work and slept on the floor. I didn't have any furniture, but laying on that floor in peace was better than laying in the bed next to a man who beat me up every time he was frustrated with life. My supervisor approved a temporary change of schedule, and I started working at an earlier time. Every night, one of my coworkers would call and let me know he would be sitting outside of the Post Office at the time I would usually be getting off work. He didn't dare to approach one of them to ask where I was.

I called my sister and asked if she would keep the kids until I got some beds and furniture. She said yes and let me know she was praying for me, and I knew they were in a safe place.

My days off came around, and I went shopping for pots and pans and dishes and got a couple of lawn chairs on sale to put in the living room. I was putting things away, and I heard a knock on my door. My heart sank. He found me was the thought that sent a wave of fear through me. I ran upstairs to the window and peeped through the blinds. It was my girlfriend, Karen, from work. She was the only person with my address. I was relieved and wondered why she didn't call first.

I went downstairs and opened the door. Karen was standing there, smiling. "I have something for you," she said. She pointed at a truck a man was driving. This is my cousin, Mack, and he had some things in storage. I told him your story, and he said you could have this furniture." That's why she didn't call before coming over; it was a surprise and a great blessing sent from the LORD.

She motioned for him to pull the truck up to the door. I was shocked to see all the furniture. They had a full-size bed, twin beds, a sofa, and a dinette set.

I told her I would pay her cousin for the furniture. She said, "No, we are giving you these things. You never have to go back." She told me she couldn't believe such a nice woman married such an evil man. "You are far away from home down here in Texas, and we are here to help you." I laughed and cried at the same time. It felt so good to know somebody cared.

I didn't know how or where the help would come from. I didn't know who or when it was going to happen. All I knew was God is faithful, and He makes a way for us when it seems there is no way to ever get out of a bad situation. I wasn't expecting help from anybody, and I was content to sit on the lawn chairs and sleep on the floor until I could save enough to get some furniture.

But God supplies all our need according to His riches, not according to when I'm going to get a paycheck. Hallelujah! I'm grateful that God is faithful! So, be encouraged no matter what you're going through. Know that He is no respecter of persons, and what He did for me He will do also for you.

Collateral Beauty Moment

The furniture that I was blessed with is just one of many ways God will provide when you become locked into His purpose for your life. The Collateral Beauty of a divorce from an abusive husband was a good thing. Over time I realized that none of the abuse was my fault. He was the one with the problem, the issues, the anger. I found the peace that surpassed all understanding and discovered the beauty that I possessed. The most important thing was that this and other experiences in my life had given me the ability to help others know they can make it out of being locked in "Ask Me How I Know."

What are some things that you need to lock in on in your own life?

Chapter 10
No More Tears
By Toni Riley

I've experienced so much *bad* treatment that I seemed to be the target for people to talk about, push around, and just treat me any kind of way. As things continued to occur, I began to feel as though I wasn't good enough for anybody to like or to care about. I began to think that love was when others treated me badly, and if they didn't, somehow, I felt worse because I must have done something to make them mistreat me. Had *no* clue of the value I held inside.

This storm began one evening in the summer of 1989. I met a gorgeous guy through some family friends, and thought *yes; he is fine*. He was dreamy, and all I wanted was to experience him in the bedroom. And what an experience. He was better than I expected, and the night didn't end until morning. Yet, I had no idea how our lives would change from one choice... a regrettably bad choice.

He left the next morning, going about his daily routine for work. I received a call while he was on break, and he was asking if I needed anything from the Pill & Puff Store. This was a thoughtful gesture, and I gave him a small list of things to bring me. In my naïve mind I was thinking, *wow, he didn't just want sex; he really likes me.* He'd told me that he wanted to help me and the kids. Of course, I believed him. Why wouldn't I?

Less than 24 hours of us meeting, he wanted to take me to meet some of his family and friends in Wisconsin. I've never known anyone who wants to introduce someone to family and friends in such a short time. I was wondering what was he up to, but went along with his request.

Once we arrived, I met two of his uncles, Joe and Charles, a few neighbors, and Joe's girlfriend. We didn't enter the house, but spent time hanging out on the porch laughing and talking with drinks in hand. Everyone was complimenting on how cute I was and that R.D. had found a "nice girl." They complimented me so much, I began to wonder what previous girls he'd dated looked like. Just as I was considering his previous girlfriends, the neighbor said, "She really is cute, R.D. Where did you find her?" Without warning, R.D. fiercely looked at me and said, "Let's *go!*"

I picked up my cup and, to my surprise, R.D. snatched it from me! Shocked filled my emotions, as I was trying to figure out what had happened, and what triggered this change in his attitude. Before I could gather my thoughts, he yelled at me to get in the car. After we'd gotten in the car, he began questioning me and telling me that I was talking too much to his family and neighbors. He accused me of being too friendly. Yet, I thought the primary reason for us going was for me to get to know his family and friends. We began the ride to his job to pick up his check, and the ride was long and tense. I didn't know what to say or how to respond to his strange and suspect behavior. Once we got out of the car, he began pushing me, and I was completely caught off guard at what was happening to me. All I knew is that I had to get away and started running down the street while others stood by and watched what was happening.

With everything in him, he was running after me and yelling for me to stop, or I would regret trying to leave him. I was thinking to myself *this fool is crazy* and at the same time willing for my feet to keep moving. As the saying goes "feet don't fail me now."

Once he caught up to me, I was thrown to the ground, and a true tussle began! I was fighting for my life. Before I knew it, he'd put an arm across my throat, and I was gasping for air. I couldn't breathe and thought I was going to die at the hands of this persuasive, suave, yet manipulative, and violent person.

To save my life, I stopped fighting back with the hopes that he would release his arm from my airway, so I could breathe again. As I began to reason with him, he started to calm down. He picked me up, and told me to get into the car and promised not to hurt me again, as long as I cooperated with him. When I looked around, all of the people who'd been outside when this fiasco started were nowhere to be seen. They'd left me to defend myself against a guy who was bigger and stronger.

At this point, I just wanted to get out of this tangled mess and be home with my children. I had *no* intentions of seeing or talking to him again. Once I got home, I quickly jumped out of the car and told him I couldn't do this anymore. Ironically, the "this" had only begun the day before with a decision that I was already regretting. I'd allowed flesh to have its way because of my desire to be with him in the bedroom. At that time, I was a sex addict and frequently making bad decisions, and he was definitely one of them.

In all of my poor decisions, this was the first time I'd dealt with someone being aggressive and abusive. I was afraid and wanted out of this situation.

The pleading and apologies began, and I didn't want to have anything to do with this man. He was out of his mind crazy if he thought I was going to continue to see him. Well, that lasted all of less than 24 hours. He called me, paged me, and soon there was a knock at the door—all I could see was a big bouquet of colorful flowers, and he was asking to come in my house. I opened the door, and he was standing there with those flowers, asking can he come in my house! I should have told him to take a long walk on a short bridge! That's what should've happened, but instead I allowed him in to talk, soon forgave him, and night turned to morning with him staying overnight. This is how forgiving can become mistaken for knowing when to just forgive, but let *go*, and get *out*!

Things were going great, and we even took a road trip to visit his mom and grandma. I was excited to be going somewhere with him and knew that since I was meeting more of his family that things were going to change, and we would be a great couple. We drove from Wisconsin to Tennessee and spent the weekend spending quality time with the people he loved. Although he went to the juke joint and got drunk, I never saw any aggressive behavior during this visit and was confident that the abuse was a one-time thing, and that he wouldn't hit, push, or kick me ever again. He was different. He was kind. He was loving.

On our time returning, we drove back to Wisconsin and, after dropping me off at home, R.D. went to spend time with his uncle; just letting them know he was back in town. I spent some quiet moments in the house before deciding to take a nap and rest from our road trip. Returning to the house drunk, R.D. dragged me out of bed and began yelling about me being tired. The fight began, and he kicked me off my feet, causing my head to hit the floor. It was always my head that got hit or pushed into the walls! Not to mention the bruises that I was always covering up to keep people from seeing my truth… my reality.

Several weeks later, my mother had a major stroke which affected her left side and caused her to lose mobility. This caused an emotional shock at a different level. Once we got her to the hospital and after many tests, we had to decide on a plan to help her recover. I was at the hospital every day visiting her while at the same time maintaining my home by getting the kids off to school, attending school myself, and working. This was a difficult time, but I had to manage because the doctors kept saying my mother would recover after therapy and treatment.

After several weeks, she'd improved and was ready to be discharged home. I was excited and looking forward to enjoying more life experiences with her. I wouldn't get those experiences. My mother died on April 3, 1989, the night before she was scheduled to come home. I was devastated and left the hospital in emotional pain, loneliness, and feeling lost. I couldn't wrap my thoughts around what had happened, yet had to gather my thoughts enough to tell my children. I called my god-sister to come over for comfort and to be with me as I told my children that their grandmother had passed away. They were sad, confused, very unhappy, and couldn't understand how I let this happen. I couldn't answer all their questions, but I remember my god-sister filling in wherever I had a loss of words.

R.D. and I went to my mother's house and my emotions erupted as the tears began to explode down my eyes. I was crying uncontrollably, as I fell across my mother's bed. To my surprise, R.D. snatched me up and told me, "Okay, she's gone now; let's *go*!" I was completely caught off guard and confused. Where was his sympathy? Why did he not understand this pain and the raw emotion I was feeling? We walked back to the house in silence with quiet tears rolling down my face. I was having a rush of different feelings because I was void of the comfort that I needed from R.D.

Later in the day, he went down in the basement, and I clumsily followed him to see what was wrong. As I turned the corner entering the basement, he punched me so hard I believe I temporarily lost my vision. He was angry that my god-sister and her husband were still at the house when we returned. He yelled, "When I tell you to get people out of the house, do what I tell you!" When I tried to respond, he jumped up and kicked me in the chest.

During this exhaustive fight, I remember falling to the floor, and he jumped on top of me and started taking off my pants to have sex. Each time as I was trying to get my bearings, he would punch me. Eventually, I just laid still until he was done. After he drifted off into a deep sleep in the basement, I went upstairs to shower and go to bed.

The next morning, he came upstairs and asked me why did I sleep upstairs??? WTW!!! Was he on another planet, or did I just have the worst nightmare in my life? "You don't remember what you did last night?" I asked. He said, "I thought I was dreaming."

After this incident, I was done. I couldn't take it anymore and decided that I was going to get rid of him one way or another. I prepared dinner and set some things in motion to literally kill him. Yes; it had gotten to the point that I wanted to take this man's life. When he came home drunk again, I knew what was planned would work, and I would be free from the abuse.

To my surprise, on this night, he was skeptical to eat the food I'd made for us to eat. To prove that nothing was wrong with his plate, I started eating it. He was then convinced that I hadn't done anything to the food, and he proceeded to eat the entire serving from his plate. Little did he know; the poison was in the middle instead of on the edges where I'd eaten.

After he finished, I had instant regret and cried like a baby. Once I pulled myself together and realized what I'd done, I knew I'd gone too far and had gotten myself into something that was taking me on a path that could cause me to be separated from my children.

I went to church to get renewed, refreshed, and restored, and somehow stayed in the relationship. One day he came home, and I heard him calling my son a punk. When I entered the room to defend my son, R.D. responded and *WHAM*!

The fight began as if we were in a heavy weight boxing ring. With a flash, he had a knife to my throat and, before I knew it, we were standing at the neighbor's door, and she refused to open it. With the knife to my throat, R.D. dragged me across the street to a phone booth and demanded that I call 9-1-1, or he would cut my throat. Reluctantly, I dialed the three numbers thinking about my children and that my life was about to be over. Who was going to raise my babies??? I had so many things going on that I wanted—*I needed*— God to show-up right away!

The police came from the side walkway yelling for R.D. to surrender. I took off running pass the police to my house, grabbed my kids, and held them tight, as we cried and comforted one another. I pressed charges, and on the court date I realized I didn't know this man at all. He had several alias names when all I knew him by was R.D. After all of this I realized I had been staying with a *total* stranger! He got three months of probation and, after staying with my brother for a while, I went home to pray over and clean it. I remember asking God to help me with asking him to leave without him trying to hurt or kill me, and He answered my prayer. I told R.D. that I had been praying for him, and it was time for him to go before one of us killed the other. He agreed; said I was absolutely right, and apologized for his actions. I never saw R.D. again, and my healing process began for me and my kids.

I ended up calling my friend (my now hubby), and he was finally free, and I was coming out of that relationship. I regretted evening falling for the same old stuff that got me into the same old moments. I can't live by myself (I had my kids to raise), I needed to be needed (I was by my kids); why won't anybody love me (my kids did). So, I got into a new relationship with Jeff, carrying all this weight; but, he was willing to go through the fire with me.

How do I really know if this man loves me, I asked myself? I really needed to go and see a professional because all the physical, emotional, and lack of spiritual help; I was pretty messed up. Yet, I kept going day after day, faking it and never making it; until one day my husband said to me, "When will you stop making me pay for those other fools?" I broke down and cried like a baby!

I had disappointed myself, my kids, and now my husband. *Where will this end?* I went to church for Bible Study and told the Lord I needed a complete overhaul!

You know what I'm talking about. Like when you backslide, or kept running from church to church, or just being offended. (Do you get where I'm going with this?) God is still, years later, putting the pieces in place for me and my husband of 25 years, 8 months, and counting. We go to the same ministry where the Word is being taught, and we are still working on our marriage, and I've learned that I am more valuable than rubies, diamonds, and pearls.

I only want to be the wife that my husband will honor and respect! The mom my children and legacy will call *blessed*! The woman who is whole again, and the daughter that God will say, "Good and faithful servant..." Women already know what your worth is, so you don't have to go looking for it on the wrong ship!

Chapter 11
Emotional Scars for Beauty Marks
by Sherri Laird-Scates

As a child I was abused and rejected by the people who were supposed to love, protect, and provide for me. I lacked the very necessaries of life, both emotionally and physically. My father, while physically present, was emotionally and financially absent. My everyday need for things like food and female hygiene products was not met. Growing up this way lead me down a path of looking for the love that I missed and the security I lacked. My relationship path was filled with abuse. I went from one relationship to another, never allowing my heart to heal or to become comfortable with getting to know me.

I graduated from high school and then got married at the age of 21. I was married for five years when my husband decided he did not want children, nor did he want to be married anymore. He literally broke my heart. I fought hard to keep the marriage but failed. I actually can't say I blame him looking back now at our marriage.

You see, I never wanted to have sex with him, as I thought sex was dirty. It was the way I was raised. My mother was not faithful to my father, and I would witness the ugly things she did with a variety of men. It affected my belief system around sex and its intended purpose. Years of counseling retrained my thinking on how I felt about me, sex, and relationships. I learned that sex was something beautiful when shared with a person you love. So, here I am at the age of 27 years old, so very broken, lost, and starting all over again.

Let me go back a bit; so, my husband asked me for a divorce. A few months later, I started seeing another man who worked for the same company as my ex-husband and I. He had a crush on me for the last few years. He worked in the Purchasing Department, and I worked in Accounts Payable. We came in contact frequently, as I handled a few of his vendors. He was a very arrogant, pushy man, and I really could not stand him. But, he would not take no for an answer. He would leave flowers on my desk and cards almost every day.

He then followed me home, so he knew where I lived. So, I started getting flowers sent to my house each week. He would not leave me alone. Finally, I broke down and went out with him. A week after my divorce was final, I found I was pregnant. My ex-husband wanted me back. He was trying very hard. I wanted to go back to my ex, but was also very hurt by him walking out on me. One of the reasons he said he was walking out of the marriage was that he did not want to have any kids. So, I did not think he would want to raise another man's baby; especially, when he did not want one with me. So, I ended up having an abortion, which happened to be on my birthday. It was one of the worst days of my life.

I was so very confused, hurt, and lost during that time. The man I was pregnant for still loved me very much and still wanted to be with me. I felt like I should stay with him and make myself fall in love with him; he was trying so hard. So, I stayed with him, and not even six months later, I became pregnant again. So, there was no way I was going to have another abortion. I felt like I was supposed to have this man's baby, or walk away from him. You sure reap what you sow. He bought me a beautiful engagement ring, asked me to marry him, but I was not in love with this man, so I would not marry him. I did end up moving in with him towards the end of my pregnancy, though, as I was afraid and thought I needed his help.

My first son was born, and he died at birth. I ended up having an emergency C-section after he died, and they were able to bring him back. He was such a beautiful baby boy—a total miracle from the Lord. So, I stayed with his dad for two more years, and then I left him. He changed drastically after our son was born. He would not allow me to go anywhere, or to spend any money. He would take all of my paychecks and tell me what to do. I was a pretty independent woman even back then, so I would stand up to him, and he did not like that.

He started hitting me, leaving bruises on me all the time. My manager at work never liked him at all. So, he helped me move out and leave him during work hours. He knew I was very afraid of him. I moved in with a girlfriend whom I used to babysit when she was little. She was 10 years younger than me. She came into my life right before my son was born. She was a lifesaver for me in so many ways. So, I lived with her for a few years. I ended up falling in love with her step-brother, who I knew from high school. He was two years older than me. I had always had a crush on him in high school, but he never even knew I was even alive until he met me at his sister's home.

We were friends for the first year. He liked my son a lot. My son seemed to love him, too. He would take my son out to see his horse all the time, take him for ice cream cones, and was trying to get me to fall for him. I just kept telling myself I was going to take time, this time, and not just go from one relationship to another. But, then I ended up falling in love with him. So, we dated for the next year. He was a funny, very handsome, well-dressed man. I was very happy until I moved out and moved back into my home. He moved in with me. It was not long after, that I realized he had a major cocaine problem. I tell you... you never know someone until you live with them.

Once I caught him and realized this, everything went downhill from there. He became extremely abusive; the worst I had ever seen. This man put me through complete hell. The worst part was that my son saw it all. He beat me all the time; I always had cracked ribs. He would continue always to hit me in the same place, so my ribs would never heal. They got to the point they would not stay in and popped out all the time.

The doctor I was seeing turned him in eventually. I would always lie and try to protect him. He would hold me down and raped me a few times. He destroyed my home with holes in the walls and doors. He would burn my personal belongings. He had manic depression and was also bi-polar. He was a very disturbed man; to this day he still is.

I ended up pregnant with his child. He beat me— would kick me in the stomach before he knew I was pregnant. I ended up in the hospital at five months and stayed there until I gave birth to my 2nd son. I was losing a lot of blood, and they could not figure out why. They found out the day I gave birth that he had kicked me so many times in the stomach, the placenta had ripped from the uterus, causing me to bleed a lot.

I gave birth to a very healthy baby boy. I eventually was able to get away from him. I had many restraining orders against him. But, he was not afraid of anyone or anything.   He ended up marrying another woman, but did the same things to her. She eventually had him served with divorce papers. The day he got the papers, he tried to kill her. My younger son was there. She was able to get away.

The cops got him, and he went to prison for a few years. She took the silent witness program. She was terrified of him. She had me subpoenaed to attend the court hearing for his sentencing. That was *so* very hard, as I had to relive all of the pain and suffering I had endured for those 11 years that I was with him. They also offered me the silent witness program, but I did not take it. I had just built a very nice home, had a great job, and I was not going to start over again! So, once he went to prison, and the trial was over, I was able to get on with my life with some sort of peace.

I went on raising my two boys as a single mother. I have never remarried. I was a pretty damaged, broken woman to say the least, but still I tried to be the best mom I knew how to be. I always wanted my boys to have all the things I never did. I wanted to give them plenty of my time, my love, and teach them morals, self-respect, and how to treat others. The lessons I have learned looking back over my life is that I realized the reason I was this way was from not having been raised with any guidance, morals, self-confidence, self-esteem, or self-worth—not much love at all. This is why I would fall apart when I would break up in my relationships; I would stay in bed for days and slip into a deep depression.

Having a man in my life was my *everything*. (In a way they were the dad I never had.) I would stay in a very toxic relationship long after I should have walked away. But, when we do this, we lose ourselves to the point of breaking. I would repeat this behavior with every relationship. I would always wonder what is wrong with me. *Why am I so weak? Why can't I be strong and walk away, never to look back?* Why couldn't I see my self-worth? It is the worst way to live like that. But, this is exactly what happens when you are raised the way I was. I was always told by my father that you are better to be seen and not heard. I was to go to my room and leave him alone. My dad always came home late from work, and he was in a bad mood; he did not want to be bothered ever! This consistent message from him made me feel that I was worthless, not significant. Why should I even be living? I would try very hard to have any relationship with my dad, but he was not interested. I never had a mother growing up either. She remarried and moved out-of-state and started a whole new family.

I pretty much raised myself along with my siblings being that I was the oldest. So, when a man comes into your life and shows you any attention, you are so desperate for love, you take it. I mean, what is a good man? What does that look like? Here you go down the wrong road. After my younger son's father went to prison, I just focused on being a mom; no more dating, no more relationships for me for the next seven years. I went back to counseling; I started working out at the gym, learning how to be happy just hanging with me. I did not know how to be satisfied without having a man in my life; I thought I needed one to complete me.

Over the years with spending time alone, I learned to like myself. I started going back to church, went to many bible studies, and attended the women's retreats each year. I must say the more I learned about GOD, the happier I became. I learned how much God loves me, and that was life-changing for me. I learned my self-worth. I can now say that I am a beautiful, strong woman, who knows what she wants in life. I know what kind of man I want, and I will not settle for anything less than a GODLY man. I can even say that if GOD does not put him in my life, then I am okay just the way I am. I am *complete* and whole with Jesus Christ!

I now travel the world, and go on mission trips. My passion is to help other hurting women to become the best version of themselves that they can be. I lead a Hurting Mom's class at my church. I start each day with Jesus. He is the only way.

Collateral Beauty

I believe there are somethings that other has told us about ourselves as children that shows up in adulthood. It may have come in the form of a statement or and action towards you. Sherri father action lead her to "be seen and not heard." This lead to feeling of not being worthy and unhealthy relationships. Do you have any thoughts places in your head as a child that has spilled over into adulthood?

Sherri did the work and begin to like herself and be content in her singleness and her time is spend working in purpose and helping others. In your own life, how have you been able to turn those words around for purpose?

Chapter 12
Glory In the Storm
by Shaffon T. Johnson

I had a life of happiness and fun with my spouse. He was a great provider, a good husband, and a good father in my eyes. We partied, traveled, and enjoyed life. We were great friends. To me, I had found the man I have always wanted. (Just like my father.)

In the beginning, he always made sure I was happy and that I had everything that I wanted. I married my best friend. As the years went by, things started to change. He became very controlling and abusive.

I experienced some physical, mental, verbal, and emotional abuse. Some people would ask, "Why didn't you leave if he was doing all these things to you?" I had no answer. All I knew was that he was my husband and the father of my children. He was a great provider and a good persuader. He was a man who took all my weaknesses and preyed on them. I went from knowing who I was to living a life for someone else. I not only was a housewife, but I was his "sleeping pill" as well.

On November 19, 2013, my life came to a halt. I felt my happy life just went crashing down. On this day, he just walked in and announced he wanted to leave as casual as requesting his favorite meal. This request came out of nowhere. I was so blindsided, I was lost for words.

His announcement came after a heated argument about living a lifestyle that is so ungodly—like that it is shameful and humiliating. Living the lifestyle is a saying that is all too unfamiliar to the general population. A term that had plagued my marriage for years; a phrase that I no longer wanted to be associated with in any way, shape, or form... a choice I regretted. I entered this lifestyle to please and try to keep him. I abandoned my own belief and self to please him.

That night was filled with tears and wine as I wept the night away. The next morning, I was awakened to him being on top of me wanting to have sex like there wasn't an argument that had taken place, or he didn't want a divorce. As his wife, I felt that I had to have sex with him no matter what. Even though that didn't stop him from leaving; he walked out the door like nothing mattered.

He didn't care who was going to be affected by this situation. He never sat down with me to discuss this or anything. This is a position I never would have thought I would be in. I was devastated, and my heart just dropped to my feet. I was wondering where this came from, and why he was doing this to us.

I became a hermit where I shut down and closed myself off to the outside world. I couldn't focus at work, nor could I be around anyone. I couldn't even go to church because I kept telling myself, *why me God? Why do I have to endure this pain? Why do my children have to endure this pain?* (So many questions to God to which I had no answers.) I was mad at God, wondering why He took everything from my children and me.

After leaving he kept coming back and forth and again, as his wife, I felt obligated to continue to be with him. I was very confused, humiliated, and all over the place, even though I knew it was wrong to continue this with him when he did not want me anymore. He did not want us, as we had three children. I felt as I was the side chick, even though I was the wife. I was being made to feel like the cubic zirconia and not the diamond that I wore as a symbol of our marriage. Finally, after speaking with friends, I realized I needed to stop because he was sending me mixed messages and making sure I stayed at my lowest. Every time I opened up my body to him, it sent me on an emotional rollercoaster. A rollercoaster that was not only going up or down, but having many twists and turns that made me feel as though I was just a piece of meat.

March of 2014, my mind told me to file for divorce, although my heart was tied to the marriage and the idea of who he was to me. I listened to my mind and finally filed for divorce. For two years, we were in the midst of court drama, which included a custody battle and all types of side chick antics. I started drinking heavily and using sex as a coping tool to get through. I lost 40 pounds in one month. I couldn't sleep at all.

The divorce went on for two years. His children were a convenience to him. After going through all of this, I went through eviction from our home and had to move out; the home I shared with him and our three children. I was heartbroken and in a financial crisis. I had no trust in men. I used things to cope with all the hurt and pain that I was enduring. I told myself I would not ever be in another relationship ever again.

After the eviction, I didn't know where my children and I were going to go. We'd had to move out of the only home my children knew. I had to find a place fast. I found my children and me a place, only to be unable to afford it.

At this point, we were homeless and living place to place. In less than a year, my children had gone from a stable two-family home to living in hotels, with friends, and with family. Finally, in July 2015, I was able to afford our very own home. In this little two-bedroom house, although it was nothing compared to my four-bedroom two-story home, my children and I found our own place, and this is when the healing process started to take place. We all started going to counseling. I started going to counseling regularly. At this point, I was able to begin to forgive my husband for all the hurt, pain, and humiliation he caused our three children and me.

In October 2015, he got sick and the side chick left him and took everything. Again, as his wife, here I come to rescue him because in the back of my mind, he was the father of my children, and he is still my husband.

Once I helped him to get back to health, we started talking to each other and having conversations without arguing. We started dating each other and seeing each other again. We cancelled the divorce process and started staying together with each other. During this period, I felt that everything was going well, and we were going in the right direction, and we were working things out, but shame on me again after eight months of being back together. Here comes the bomb... he left once again. The feelings of despair came back all over.

I had gone with him to his doctor's appointment, and afterwards we went to breakfast. It was there that he told me we weren't working out, and it wasn't going to work, and that he was seeing someone else. The complexity, humiliation and, again, I was all over the place, but he never had any interest in getting back together.

I felt as there was no light to this tunnel. It was like I was just his rebound because I was convenient, and still his wife, and he knew my weakness. I often contemplated the things I had lost. I was so caught up with the past, not allowing myself to move forward and open a path for the future. I had a lot of resentment for the loss of my spouse, the material things, and the comfortability of the type of life I lived. I had scar tissue that needed to be broken up; it was like having fog impeding my vision. I feared letting my guard down, opening my heart, and letting life present itself. I was focusing on the things I couldn't control. I had to realize that pain doesn't last forever if you do not let it; there was light at the end of the tunnel.

I thought I was good with forgiving him—all the hurt and pain he brought me—but I had to tell myself that this is who he is as a person, and you cannot let this bad thing push you back into that depressed and withdrawn stage. I had to learn to be able to forget the past, to be able to move forward with my future, and that included everything that had good and bad in it. I had to be ready to embrace the new and release all of the bad things I experienced in my marriage. I had to learn a different type of coping skill like meditation to be able to put all my energy into forgetting all the awful things. I had to start getting back to know who I was and going further in my career.

I started back to school and surrounding myself with positive individuals who kept me in a place that was grounded and made sure I was on track with the things I was battling—through all this complexity, hurt, pain, shame, homelessness, bitterness, and humiliation. I felt like I lost everything, and I continuously thought about it. And every time I thought about everything, I felt depressed. But the return of hope came back when I remembered to read the bible such as, Lamentations 3:19-24, "The LORD is all I have," and so in Him, I put my hope. Also, in the book of Psalms 27:14, "Wait on the LORD; be of good courage, and he shall strengthen thine heart; wait, I say, on the LORD." As I waited on the LORD, He strengths my heart."

Also, Psalms 147:3, "He heals the brokenhearted and binds up their wounds." Upon reading some of these scriptures, I learned that if I had the strength and courage, then the LORD would strengthen my heart back to whole. And make sure that all the heartbreaking I received from my heart would be healed. There are times we struggle with sins in our lives holding grudges, unwilling to give, love, etc., but God has a way of transforming and changing us from some of the deepest, darkest, places in our lives. By his grace, we are healed.

When it comes to deciding to forgive, according to Psalms 25:4-5, we must seek guidance. It is a good idea to wait on God to give you the direction and timing. While waiting, we can take a look at our heart, asking the Lord to call out any wrongs that are there and, if the Lord gives you an answer, you must repent or do what it takes to make it right. Any transgressions must be dealt with for us to be able to heal.

When in search of direction, we must make sure we listen to God's words very patiently and effectively. I know that being patient can be very hard on us; especially, when we are full of emotions because it is so easy for us to have the focus on all the pain when everything is falling apart. There was a point I was so mad at God that I kept asking myself, "Why me, Lord?" But even though we are upset, we need to remember that God loves us. We must pay attention to the love that is unconditional that He gives unto us. So, no matter how mad we get at Him, scream at Him, ask a thousand questions, we must still remember that His love is still there. God allowed me to recover my heart and soul even though I despised my spouse. I was a woman scorned with a vast ocean of anger and bitterness in her heart. Divorce leaves a void and an empty place where companionship and happiness should reside. Add to that the pain our children suffered because of the breakup of their parents and leaving the only home they knew.

Eventually, I met a new man, and this was when my Collateral Beauty came into effect. This was when I knew I had made peace with my past relationship. I was at a point in my life where I was able to trust a man again, and to know what it was like to be loved without there being an agenda behind saying, "I love you." I learned to remain true to myself and my conviction. I was open about my past and let him know upfront that the lifestyle will not be part of our future.

The new man doesn't allow my past to cloud his judgment of the person I am now. I learned never to give a man so much control where you lose all your own identity or self-worth, being able to have an opinion, and to never do anything beyond my beliefs. I would never allow myself to get to a position where I no longer knew myself and was living for someone else. I learned to open up and not hold my emotions in. I learned that forgiveness is the key. Without it I would not be able to move forward with my life. We need to change and recognize our faults, as well as our values. In seeking this change, you must first forgive. Forgive so you may heal. Once you begin to heal, the change will come, and you will start growing. Forgiveness will slowly change your beauty from within. You will leave behind all the hurt, pain, bitterness, and humiliation as GOD's Word will be a continuous guide. I had to stop focusing on what I lost and start focusing on the future that was ahead for my children and me.

Once my prayers are answered, I must continue to pray during good and bad times. According to the Bible, Mark 11:26, "But if you do not forgive, neither will your Father who is in heaven forgive your trespasses." We all know we make mistakes, and everyone we encounter will not always be good to us, but we must make sure we have forgiveness.

I felt like a woman scorned, where I held a grudge, and I was irate. I was so hurt where I couldn't even have a discussion with this man. Once the forgiveness came, the joy and happiness came. I was able to have all my blessings come about in my life. I had to find peace, relief of stress, all types of emotions, such as anger and hurt. I found my solace in God's word while seeking healing, loving myself, forgiveness, and loving God as He loves me.

Chapter 13
Personal Growth is A Choice
by Pamela Jones Smith

Have you ever felt like you were stuck on a treadmill, going nowhere? Just enduring life and doing the same thing day-after-day without any success? Life has a way of happening in such a way that we don't make progress because of various reasons. Some of the reasons are financial, fear, concerned about what others will say, lack of support, and no clear plan, or guidance. But hey, this treadmill experience doesn't have to last forever; you can get off at any time. The choice is yours to begin enjoying your life to the fullest. How do I know this to be true? Because I was tired of running, yet going nowhere. I am very confident that your life can change for the better and be unrecognizable.

As a pregnant teen, I'd become a statistic; make that a two-time statistic. My first precious little girl was only with us a few hours. But in those hours, she brought us much light, love, and joy. I like to say she was too perfect for this world. During this time of loving and grieving her at the same time, I needed comfort and the love of family and friends. At this time, I began to learn the importance of one of my best "Pam's Pearls": It's ok to just sit in silence and to not have an answer. It's ok to sit in silence and just be. It's ok to just sit in silence and not say a word. Silence and your presence are comforting. Silence can be golden in this situation.

A year later, I was a teenage mom once again in September; my beautiful baby girl was born, my angel. The following May, against all the odds, I graduated from high school. This practical tip would lead to another Pam's Pearls of not allowing others to put their limiting beliefs on you. I had to stop listening to people say that my life was ruined, and that I would never graduate from high school. I couldn't focus on the naysayers, or I would easily give up and begin believing what I was hearing day in and day out. Even when they didn't say anything out loud, the nonverbal communication spoke volumes, and I'd been written off as a failure. However, I was determined not to allow anyone to define my journey and future, and neither should you. We should all be determined to reach our goals, and as we all know, there is no stopping a determined person.

I married my daughter's father in June 1980, one week after graduation and moved to Phoenix, Arizona.

Talk about getting out of your comfort zone and stepping into the unknown. This was a defining moment of growing in my life because I didn't know anything about living in a big city. Oh, did I mention that it was July when I moved to Phoenix? It was scorching hot as my new husband, daughter, my parents, and mother-in-law drove into the blistering desert to begin our new life. Although it was hot and difficult to breathe, starting this new journey was a breath of fresh air. With this experience comes another of Pam's Pearls: a humid environment requires plenty of water and maintaining an abundant supply of popsicles in the freezer.

Being from a small town in the mid-west, I dared to take a leap and move to a place I didn't have any family or friends. There was only one person I knew in Phoenix. That was my husband's uncle. Being raised going to church, I was determined to find a place I could continue to serve and be among other Believers.

I attended a church, and by tradition they asked visitors to stand, state their name, and church. Honoring the tradition, I stood and provided my information, and to my surprise, Pastor L. L. Smith informed me that we were "kin folk." I called my father, who verified this information, and I was delighted. Obviously, this became my home church, and I realized that when I'm intentional about my desired next level, I'm unstoppable. You can be unstoppable, too!

I desired to go to college to obtain a degree in counseling. However, I was a newly married wife with a daughter in a new city, and so begins the journey of stepping off my path onto the treadmill of going nowhere. I compromised and settled for cosmetology school instead. Although I was talented in my skills of bringing beauty to others through hair, it wasn't my passion. Deep down in my heart, the burning desire of encouraging and adding value to others still existed. The flame wouldn't burn out for what I knew I was meant to do to help others. The truth of the matter is, no matter how great I made their hair look, my clients didn't even realize their hair didn't look like the picture they gave me. I genuinely believe they came back every week because they liked being encouraged.

As I was building my new life and home, it appeared to everyone that I was enjoying life. Now don't misunderstand what I'm saying because I was truly happy. My life was filled with even more joy a couple of years later when I had my son, my precious baby boy. I was living an amazingly good life, but I wasn't enjoying life. You know it is a big difference between being happy and enjoying your life. Being happy is based on circumstances; enjoying your life is based on operating in your full potential. We can be happy and living a good life, but if we aren't walking in our purpose or operating in our full potential, we can feel as though we are on the treadmill of life. At moments, the treadmill is at high speed, and it seems as if we're trapped running in place going nowhere and just enduring in life.

Fast forward 18 years later because I began to experience what I thought was the worst thing that could ever happen to me. Because of a divorce, I was thrust out of my comfort zone once again. I instantly lost the security of having a husband, a protector, and a provider, also a two-parent home raising our children. I was now homeless with two children to take care of on my own.

Determined I would not be defeated, I stood on God's Word. His promise to me was in Psalms 27:1. *The Lord is my light and salvation; Whom shall I fear? The Lord is the strength of my life; f whom shall I be afraid?* Salvation means He keeps me from failure, harm, loss, and destruction. He saves and protects me.

I was intentional about setting goals to move forward. So, I created and executed an action plan, and one year later, I purchased my very own townhouse with only my name on the deed. While going through this challenging time, I learned that it was okay to take time to get upset and cry over the loss. I learned the importance of taking time to pause and reflect on learning the lesson and being firm in saying goodbye.

Through this divorce, I gained more of Pam's Pearls of not allowing bitterness to set in and define who I was. I had to learn that I was still a fantastic individual, and

I wasn't going to let anyone take that away from me. I embraced journaling and created a new game plan for my new life because I instantly become a single mother. I thanked God every day for giving me an excellent support system. They graciously accepted the challenge of helping me overcome the obstacles I was facing.

The goal-setting led to a mindset shift, as I was growing personally. I was determined, intentional, and committed to learn and grow in the critical areas and make the adjustments, releasing all limiting beliefs.

The new journey began with a new job at a call center, and one day as I was sitting at work, I realized I was just enduring. I decided that I'd had enough! I'd had enough of sitting in the same area day after day! I'd had enough of reading the same sales script to customers day in and day out, and I'd definitely had enough of having a headset attached to my head. It got to the point where I began referring to my headset as my un-detachable umbilical cord. I soon realized I couldn't move any further than the cord if I didn't make adjustments. *I felt trapped!*

The "aha" moment came like a bolt of lightning. A fire was set ablaze inside of me, and I knew at that moment I needed another mindset shift. It occurred to me that my environment was not going to change as long as I continued to settle. I instantly changed the way I was thinking about my current situation. Pam's Pearls:

sometimes it's necessary for you to change your mental environment, even before you can change your physical position. I knew I needed a change from my current work environment, but I had to be strategic about it. Don't forget; I had two beautiful children depending on me.

How was I expecting to be able to do the same mundane routine every day and hope to see a different result? How was I expecting things to change without making purposeful changes within myself? It was pure insanity to think that things would change if I didn't take any action for them to change.

As each day passed, I became more and more desperate to experience change and personal growth. As my desperation began to mount, my determination grew stronger and became a force to be reckoned with because the flame of the fire continued to burn to be successful.

I was in need of a realistic and specific action plan for success, my attitude as the 1st thing I can transform. You can't always change your situation right away, but you can change your position and how you respond to a job instantly. When you have a positive attitude it, makes it easier to respond to any situation you may find yourself in. I started being thankful and changing negative thoughts to positive thoughts. While I desired new jobs, I was grateful for the excellent pay and benefits. I began to reflect and realized that I'd started dressing down, which wasn't my character. With this reflective moment, I took immediate action and started dressing up for work because this lifted my mood. I was determined and committed to change my situation from down and out, to lead and succeed. I had some self-evaluation and improvements to make. It wasn't just for me to act and dress for success, but I had to shift into a positive mindset that would overflow in every area of God's plan for my life. What's His plan? I'm glad you asked; "For I know the plans I have for you," declares the LORD. "Plans to prosper you and not to harm you, plans to give you hope and a future" Jeremiah 29:11.

That was the groundbreaking first step to an intentional and positive "new me." With each successful step, I began the next actions toward success. I started going to women's conferences and workshops; I also started reading more books on being positive. During the season of being in full-fledge forward movement of being the best version of myself I could be and growing every day, in this new chapter of letting my light shine and enjoying life, I met my current husband.

As a result, I was once again thrust out of my comfort zone. Why? Because his character is the complete opposite of mine. He has a dry sense of humor, is very calm, and always goes with the flow. My sense of humor is upbeat, and I love spontaneity. He's taught me that I don't always have to know all the details before I launch into something new. In this marriage, the union predestined by God, and this journey, we've both grown personally and learned how to bring balance into our relationship.

Our like-mindedness leads us to laser focus on our area of growth: finances. We started with finances and went back to basics. If it wasn't a basic need for survival, we turned it off or got rid of it— including cable, cell phone, eating out, and two vehicles. I became creative in cooking our meals to allow for leftovers at work for lunch and the next day's dinner. We carpooled to work and soon realized the sacrifice being made had quick results. The payoff was *great*! Not only did we begin to have more quality time together, but we also became debt free, began a rainy-day savings account, and were able to purchase a home.

I had great potential that was locked inside of me, ready to be unleashed, and personal growth was my road to it. After overcoming limiting beliefs and a self-sabotaging mentality, I completed a program and became a certified personal growth life coach. I am very passionate about working with others in realizing their full potential and achieving their next level of success, taking them from enduring life to enjoying life.

Along the journey, I accepted several invitations to speak at women's events, conferences, and workshops. The motivating factor for me has been my favorite scriptures: 1 Corinthians 2:9. "Eye has not seen, nor ear heard, nor entered into the heart of man, the things which God has prepared for those who love him." My perception changed when God showed me I am the answer to many people's prayers, and He wants to use me to help his daughters.

Being transparent and sharing my story lead to the realization that my Collateral Beauty was there the whole time as "Pam's Pearls." As life changes came, I was about to find my purpose by always embracing the lessons and blessing of the situation. I learned to leap off that treadmill.

Collateral Beauty

Pamela used goal-setting as a tool to push past her own limiting beliefs. Limiting beliefs are the messages we replay in our head that tells us we are unable to achieve something or negative thinking.

Have you ever had a situation that made you feel trapped as if an un-detachable umbilical cord held you back from a dream or a desire?

Chapter 14
My Collateral Lessons
by: Sandi D. Johnson

Divorce is such a small word, but it is one in which changes lives. It represents the death of a relationship, a change of lifestyle, an empty other side of the bed, and so much more. The word divorce rocks the whole world of both adults and children. This word has changed my world two times.

As a preschooler, this word crept into my world. This word was not in my vocabulary as a 4-year-old, but hearing it would make my heart fall to my stomach. This word would bring about instant tears. This word caused us to move multiple times, and no longer have a Daddy in my home. How did this word become part of my story and create a hole in my heart for many years?

My parents married at a very young age and had three beautiful little girls. As children, the inner working of their relationships was not our business, and they never shared with us. Even as adults, my mother refused to share the why behind the marriage failure. This was done to protect the parental relationship with my Father. So, that relationship is just based on his actions and not her words. This lead to being raised in a single-parent household where my mother, with the help of a robust support system, was able to raise us up in the 1990's in inner-city Detroit. At the time Detroit was deemed the Murder Capitol of the U.S.A., and organizations were formed to fight against the number of children who were murdered in the city on a daily bases. My mother fought against the odds and raised three college-educated women.

Now, back to my first divorce as a child. I clearly remember the day we left my Dad and riding in the car with my aunt, as we pulled away from the place we called home. From there we moved around; I attended a different school for Kindergarten through 2nd grade every year. My paternal grandparents were a crucial part of our support system. We ended up living with them for some time. Yes; my mother was living with her ex-husband's, parents. My grandparents purchased a home for us and provided a stable place for us to call home. So, starting in third grade, I lived in the same house until high school graduation.

The day we moved into Marlowe Street, our home, it was so exciting. It was as if this house was made for us. The upstairs had three bed and dressers built into the walls with a playroom up front—a perfect place for our toy kitchen and baby dolls. My mother's and younger brother's rooms were downstairs. It had a finished basement and was the perfect little home for us. No more renting and moving around, but an actual place to call home. The block was mostly two-parent households with only two other single mothers on the street.

That word just keeps creeping back up. "Your parents are divorced." Even having one neighbor call and tell my sister she did not have a dad. We spent most weekends at my paternal grandmother's house, and she would talk to us about our feelings and verbalize the hurts. Her words would bring about some temporary relief, and she was able to fix some situations.

It was not until my senior year of high school that a mental light bulb went on about coming from a broken home—a "broken home." My family had never been one of those found on a sitcom like *The Cosby Show*. I only had that one memory of leaving and had no recollection of dinner together, family movie night, or any other occasion. I was missing something that I never had. The life in a "broken home" was all I knew. It was as if with that realization all the pain I carried melted away like an ice cube on a hot Texas day.

All I could recall was the joke sessions that took place in our dining room, the early morning Saturday clean-up sessions, the daily dinner my mother cooked, playing dodge ball outside, and doing the MC Hammer on the lawn as a family. The love and discipline were extended on a daily bases.

The realization that my home really was not broken came. Broken is something that is damaged, not in its original state. According to society, we were a fragmented family due to my dad not being in the home. That decision my mother made in her life to be single and to walk away from the marriage led to her wholeness. This wholeness in her life better equipped her to parent and live a full life. So, the question may have to be asked do you stay fragmented in an unhealthy relationship, or leave creating a "broken" but whole home?

Fast forward to my early 40's, I had the desire to be married, and it just had not happened for me. My three children were all in high school, and here I was facing an empty nest and still single. I had a college friend who I spoke to on regular bases over the years. He decided to come to visit during the 4th of July holiday, and by Thanksgiving we were married. You are probably like, what?! That was fast. Yes; the 4th of July things went so well, he asked me to marry him. You see in the words of Destiny's Child, "I Catered to Him." In doing so, I set a false expectation that all of his needs would be met, and any of mine would be secondary.

While walking down the aisle, I felt no excitement or butterflies in my stomach. It was strictly my desire to be married and be able to have legal sex in the eyes of God. I put my all into my marriage because I had made a commitment before God. This included cooking every day and working two jobs. He relocated to Texas to marry me. Once he was in Texas, the job search was difficult. I know he had some legal trouble in the past; it was just a lot more extensive than what I was led to believe. Job offers came and were recanted when his background report came back. This happened about two times.

I would try to pour into him and encourage him... like thinking of other legal ways to generate income for him. I found myself drained. One time, out of frustration, I reached out to someone who I felt was wise. He advised me just to *stop* and allow him to step up and be the person I needed in my life. This friend said he honestly doubted he had the ability, but I needed to be both still and quiet. This is what I did.

At one point, he went days without even taking a shower. The Lord spoke to me and said, "Treat him as if he has an illness." So, I was sweet to him and just mentioned it to him. He went to shower while I fixed dinner. Again, catering to him.

Remember the long rap sheet, well a lot of it was for domestic violence. We never fought, or got out of control.

We would just discuss and move on. One time, he came after me but caught himself. I guess his anger management skills kicked in.

Although the relationship never became physically violent, it was emotionally abusive.

From our honeymoon on, he avoided having sex with me. The level of rejection this caused was unspeakable. Remember my reasons for getting married? Yes; to have legal sex. I had more sex single than in my marriage. He told me to go find someone I could have sex with, and that he was not attracted to me. These words from the man who had just vowed to love me to death do us part seared a hole in my soul that only God was able to heal.

He left shortly after that to get a job in a state that accepted "backgrounds." I was still holding on, and he appeared to be too until he no longer needed my help. At that point, while intoxicated, he told me he never loved me, and I was subpar, and he deserved better for himself. The divorce papers were printed. I completed them and filed on August 21, 2015. What would seem like a simple divorce was not so, as he refused to sign the papers. By this time, he had lost his job, leaving me with no valid address to have the divorce papers served to him. All the while, he was posting on social media pictures of his new girlfriend, and then later returned to his former girlfriend, all along refusing to sign the divorce papers.

So, this is when my crazy starts. I contacted the former girlfriend to help facilitate getting the papers signed. They had been together for years before our marriage, and now were back together. It was so unfair that I would be the only Mrs. She too should have the opportunity to be his wife, and if his love were true, he would sign the divorce papers. Still, no signed documents, and she got mad at me saying I could just run an ad in the newspaper, since I could not serve him if I really wanted the divorce.

I began to just pray for my freedom from this marriage. My prayer was answered on December 29, 2015 when the signed and notarized papers were in my mailbox. On New Year's Eve, I was set free and went into 2016 a single woman.

This was a painful blessing. It was a real time of growth and learning what marriage was really about. Marriage is hard; especially, when both parties are not fully committed. I learned that sex should not be the focus, but the companionship and purpose.

My next and last will line up with the purpose of my life. I know if I had of stayed married, I would have been very emotionally and physically depleted that there would be no "Living Life on Purpose," no Facebook Live broadcasts, no books, and EnVision Your Life L.L.C. would not exist.

Most importantly, I learned to ask my Father in heaven; I never prayed about His will but simply did my own will. It just was all so perfect. We had known each other for years. This was such a fantastic love story. We "vibed" well together. The sex was great and on and on, but never once did I even pray about marrying him, or seek counsel from my pastor. It took me three years to start dating again. I am back at it with some scars from Collateral Damage and the wisdom that came with the Collateral Beauty.

About the Authors
Sandi D. Johnson
Vision Coach | Author | Entrepreneur

Sandi D. Johnson is a Dream Keeper, author, vision coach and motivational speaker. Her simple motto of "set a goal, achieve that goal and move on to the next goal" has been the driving factor in her success. Her life's goal is to merge her faith, gifts, passion, purpose and education to help others "Live Life on Purpose," which is the name of her social media broadcasts.

She has successfully raised three children as a single parent, overcoming many obstacles and refusing to be a statistic. Sandi uses these experiences to inspire others to be "too tough to quit" in life. Sandi is the creator and local host of the Annual "I Have a Dream" Vision Board Experience. This annual event is hosted in several cities concurrently. The women who participate leave empowered with a visual life plan. The overwhelming response to this event led to the formation of "Envision

Your Life, L.L.C." These customized vision board experiences will give participants a clear direction for life while laughing, networking, and developing a victory plan. She has conducted vision board experience for government agencies, universities, schools, businesses, and private events.

Additionally, Sandi has co-hosted "My Story, My Journey" Women's Retreat for the past five years. This is a weekend were participants explore the purpose of their journey and how these experiences can help them move forward in their purpose.

She may be contacted at **info@sandidjohnson.com.**

Subscribe to her website at **www.sandidjohnson.com**

Shaundale Rénā

Entrepreneur | Bestselling Author | Editor

Shaundale Rénā is the Owner and Chief Executive Officer of All in A Day's Work Consulting. She holds a bachelor's degree in Computer Information Systems from Grambling State University and a certification in Technical Writing from the University of Texas at Arlington. Shaundale Rénā is the author of *Once Broken, Now Blessed* (2009), as well as a contributing author of *If Only I Knew Then What I Know Now* (2017), which debuted at #16 on Amazon under Self-Help/Self-Esteem, and *Collateral Beauty* (2019). More recently she is the creator of *With the EXes! Talk Radio Show* and can be heard every Monday as the unfiltered, captivating, and witty Stony Rhodes. She is also an Independent Sales Consultant of Paparazzi Accessories. For more info visit

www.withtheEXes.com or. **www.StonysGems.com**

Dr. Monica Debro, DNP, MSN, RN

Entrepreneur | Author | Life Coach

Dr. Monica Debro, owner of Love Yourself to Life™, is a leader who is transforming the lives of women through inspirational writings, events, and speaking engagements. She is the host and keynote speaker for the Love Yourself to Life™ workshop. Dr. Debro also hosts the Always Wear Your Tiara™ event in which women have received intimate breakthroughs in their personal and professional lives. As a practicing Life Coach, Dr. Debro engages in life-changing conversations and action plans to help women embrace the essence of who they are and not allow the past to interfere with their future. She is a member of the National Coalition Against Domestic Violence and has been a guest speaker at several community violence awareness events. She is the author of *Broken Believer No More* and *Love Yourself to Life™*. Dr. Debro is also a co-author of two books: *Grace to Recover: How to Divorce Hurt, Addiction, and Overcome Trials with the Power of a Loving God* and *Collateral Beauty*.

To contact Dr. Monica visit:
www.loveyourselftolife.co

LaSonya Thomas
Entrepreneur | Author | Nurse

Sonya Thomas is a graduate of the Detroit public school system, 1983. She received her diploma in nursing from Henry Ford Hospital School of Nursing in 1991. Ms. Thomas received a Bachelor of Nursing at the University of Detroit Mercy in 2015.

Sonya is active in church: she sings in the choir, assists with communion, and is the former leader over the Praise Dance Ministry. She loves to travel and has been to various parts of the world, including Paris, France, Italy (the Vatican), and Spain to name a few.

Sonya loves to cook and entertain family and friends; the highlight of the year is her infamous first party. Sonya is the oldest daughter of Willie Joe and Frances Yvonne Thomas; she is the sister of five siblings. Her favorite saying is by Dr. Martin Luther King Jr., "The ultimate measure of a man is not where he stands in moments of comfort and convenience, but where he stands at times of challenge and controversy."

Sherry Peak

Radio Show Host | Author | Motivational Speaker

Sherry Peak is a native of Anderson, Indiana and is the Executive Director for The Anderson Impact Center, a recognizable community leader, Co-Producer for the Real People Real Voices Television Show, and the host of the Share With Sherry Talk Radio Show. Sherry has an MBA with a specialization in Business Management, BSA in Accounting, and an AAS in Business Administration. Her career includes working in nonprofit management and social services for over 20 years teaching, training, and coaching to individuals to realizing a better quality of life through education, empowerment, and entrepreneurship. Sherry has received numerous awards and has been featured in various media outlets for her outstanding work in her career field.

As an inspiring and innovative leader who is committed to personal and professional development, Sherry welcomes opportunities to learn from and share with others cutting edge strategies and solutions to achieving personal and professional success.

Danielle Reneé

Entrepreneur | Author | Insurance Broker

Danielle Reneé is a licensed and ordained minister, an author, an entrepreneur, a licensed Insurance Broker, and Owner of Divine Customized Headstone Company. Blessed with a warm-hearted personality and a heart to serve others, Danielle boasts over three decades of involvement in helping and serving people. An ordained minister for more than 20 years, Danielle's business of working with people encompasses grooming and ministering. As a licensed beautician, her mindset for helping people rubs off on her work as a beautician, assisting women to feel beautiful from inside-out. In every way and with every opportunity, she gets to help people in all aspects of their lives. Danielle takes the time to listen and give Godly advice to help people tap into the best versions of themselves. A supportive mother to five beautiful daughters and grandmother, in her capacity, Danielle finds great satisfaction in seeing people live happily and soulfully. Her previous works include: *A Mommy's Love Affair, Prophetically Spoken, A Book of Powerful Petitions and Crying Out Loud,* and *Not Being Heard.*

Felicia Kay Wilkerson

Entrepreneur | Author | Actress

Felicia is a native of Fort Worth, Texas. She is a loving wife, mother, and grandmother. She is also a Believer, an educator, an author, an actress, a life coach, an inspirational speaker, a humanitarian, and an entrepreneur. Felicia is founder of Our Legacy Speaks, under which she is an Author, a Transformational Speaker, a Life Coach, and a Consultant. Felicia is also a talk show host and hopes to soon have her own television program. She has been a professional actress for over 20 years in local theaters and film productions. Her dream is to write and perform in movies and plays that bring awareness to family and social issues, biographical films, provide voiceovers for animated films, and much more!

Felicia is a faithful member and licensed missionary of Holy Tabernacle Church of God in Christ where she has served for 21 years. She desires to help hurting people everywhere and says she can and will make a difference by living and leaving a legacy by building lives, one life at a time.

Catalina Hernández

Entrepreneur | Author | Educator

Catalina Hernández is an Author of Chicana literature and poetry, focusing on her experience as a bicultural woman to empower the voice of minority women and the borderland experience. She is an educational consultant and educator in the North Texas area.

She was born and raised in Texas with deep roots in the Rio Grande Valley. She is an Army veteran and a seasoned educator having worked with both migrant and immigrant communities on the Texas-Mexico border, San Antonio, Boston, and the North Texas areas. She is a published writer, presenter, and advocate for English Learners. Her passion in writing inspires the creation of rich resources for teachers and students to deepen their love for literature through the lens of poetry and cultural expression.

To purchase or to learn more about Catalina's writing, please visit her website at www.cathernandez.org where you can correspond with her and keep up with her latest releases.

Para comprar u obtener más información sobre los escritos de Catalina, síganla en su sitio web, <u>www.cathernandez.org</u>, donde puede comunicarse con ella y mantenerse al día con su último lanzamiento.

Ava Marie
Entrepreneur | Author | Minister

AVA MARIE is the proud mother of three children and has four grandchildren. Her family is her motivation, her passion, and her *why*. She is a dynamic, inspirational speaker, a minister and teacher of biblical principles, practices, and truths. She is a counselor for both married and singles with a special heart for ministry to children.

Ava is the Founder and CEO of Ava's Love, LLC, a multi-faceted company created to help others achieve victory over situations and circumstances they thought could never be overcome. Ava's Love, LLC helps people learn to speak up and succeed to overcome the effects of abuse. They provide safe and confidential counseling sessions, information for safe housing, and other resources that fit the needs of the individual.

Ava is the author of the upcoming book, "Reflections: From Devastation to Celebration." This book chronicles her journey to recovery from domestic violence, molestation, incest, rejection, divorces, PTSD, severe depression, and many more of life's critical moments. It's real, relational, relevant, and a great testimony of how the love of God and applying His principles of life can turn tragedy into triumph.

She is a gifted, talented, sincere, open, honest, anointed for the work, and passionate about helping others find their purpose and achieve it. Once you've met her, you'll never forget this phenomenal woman!

Toni Riley

Author | Speaker | Wife & Mother

Toni Riley was born in Milwaukee, Wisconsin. She was a single mother of three until she married Jeffery and was blessed with two additional children. She devoted her time to raising her now adult children, whose ages range from 44 to 36 years old. Family is everything to Toni, and you will find her going to family movie nights and hosting family dinners.

As a member of Faith Christian Church, Toni has served in many capacities, including the choir where you will find her occasionally leading a song. Currently, she assists the church in duplicating the sermon CD's to facilitate the spreading of the Gospel. As an empty nester, Toni has decided to refocus on her goals and has enrolled in South Mountain Community College where she is currently pursuing an associate's degree in both Art and Science in Web Development & Graphic.

When Toni is not enjoying her 10 beautiful grandchildren, who range in age from 27 to 6 years old, she enjoys bowling, reading, and music—especially, singing. Toni's dream is to speak to students worldwide about bullying and what it does to people. She has a passion for motivating the lonely, disheartened, and disappointed. Toni loves bringing joy to people and finds joy even in the rough moments.

Joy Jones-Reed

Author | Speaker | Entrepreneur

Joy is an educator, wife, and mother who loves making a difference in the lives of others. Through the years, Joy had to navigate her way through some very tough, life-changing experiences. Fortifying such resiliency and tenacity as only she could, Joy was determined not to pin the blame on God for the hurtful and tragic trials that arose in her life to try her faith.

In 2017, she did an article with Making Headline News and also appeared on the Sherry Bronson Show Television show. Joy has done various speaking engagements, is an up-and-coming author, and is in the process of starting her first non-profit entitled POWER UP. POWER UP will service those individuals who are stuck in grief or trauma, guiding them back to our power source to POWER UP on the Word of God. She is undoubtedly walking in her purpose, as she currently resides in Mansfield, TX.

Sherri Laird-Scates

Author | Missionary | Entrepreneur

Sherri Laird-Scates is a native of Arizona. She was raised in Phoenix until the age of 11 and relocated to Chandler where she currently resides as a single mother of two beautiful boys. Sherri has been employed by Intel Corporation for the past 20 years and works in Real Estate part-time. She is active in church and leads a Hurting Mom's group, which aims to help mothers deal with choices their children have made with drugs, cutting, and incarceration from a Biblical perspective.

Sherri enjoys and has led others on several mission trips to Africa and Haiti where she shares life lessons, so others do not have to live them. She is on fire for her Lord and Savior and daily picks up her cross to carry it. Her favorite scripture is Proverbs 3:5-6

Trust in the Lord with all your heart,
And lean not on your own understanding;
In all your ways acknowledge Him,
And He shall direct your paths.
Proverbs 3:6 (NKJV)

Shaffon Johnson

Author | Accountant | Entrepreneur

Shaffon Johnson is from a small town called Dermott, Arkansas and now resides in Bedford, Texas. Shaffon is a single mother of three children. She received her bachelor's degree in Business Administration, majoring in Accounting. She has been in her career field for over 10 years now.

Just a few years ago, Shaffon had to navigate her way through some very tough, life-changing experiences. Fortifying such resiliency and tenacity as only she could, Shaffon remained steadfast and was determined not to give up or put any blame on God for the hurtful events that arose in her life to try her faith. She is a strong woman who is currently walking in her purpose. With God on her side, Shaffon made the remarkable decision to go back to school to earn her master's degree, receiving a master's in science and majoring in Accounting. In doing so, she was the winning recipient of the VFW Auxiliary scholarship fund. But wait... Shaffon Johnson is not just an Accountant! She is also a tax professional, a consultant for financial strategies, math and accounting tutor, and now a co-author of a book. Shaffon is definitely a strong-willed woman and a real example of what it means to overcome adversities while fulfilling life's dreams, not letting anything hold her back.

Pamela Jones Smith
Author | Speaker | Entrepreneur

Pamela Jones Smith is the founder of Pamhasfavor, LLC in Surprise, Arizona. Pam's passion is to encourage and support women in reaching their full potential and being totally whole in every area. Pam's emphasis is helping women unleash the greatness inside of them through personal growth. She has invested over 25 years empowering women to enjoy life, rather than just endure it. Pam is also a leading performer in a fortune 500 company. She is married to her husband, Odell. When she is not coaching, speaking, or mentoring, she can be found spending time with her grandchildren and traveling with her husband.

Pam has overcome her own obstacles of limited beliefs and self-sabotaging mentality. She is also a John Maxwell certified coach, speaker, and trainer through.

www.ingramcontent.com/pod-product-compliance
Lightning Source LLC
Chambersburg PA
CBHW071218090426
42736CB00014B/2877